From a bag of chips to cod confit

A TOUR OF TWENTY ENGLISH SEASIDE RESORTS

From a bag of chips to cod confit

A TOUR OF TWENTY ENGLISH SEASIDE RESORTS

PAUL DOE

From a bag of chips to cod confit: a tour of twenty English seaside resorts

Published by The Conrad Press Ltd. in the United Kingdom 2023

Tel: +44(0)1227 472 874

www.theconradpress.com

info@theconradpress.com

ISBN 978-1-915494-71-9

Typesetting and Cover Design by: Charlotte Mouncey, www.bookstyle.co.uk

The Conrad Press logo was designed by Maria Priestley.

Printed and bound in Great Britain by Clays Ltd, Elcograf S.p.A.

For Mandy
for her love and patience

Contents

CHAPTER ONE

I do like to be beside the seaside

*Don't grow up too quickly,
lest you forget how much you love the beach*

Michelle Held, author

Why does the seaside hold such a special place in the hearts of the British? Is it the lure of the sea, whether a choppy grey or a still deep blue, the pleasure of the cliff-edge walk or the stroll along a seafront lined with colourful candy-floss stalls and bustling fish and chip shops. Perhaps it is the beach, sand in your shoes, a bucket and spade for the children and the sun on your back. Or the thrills and spills of the funfair, the excitement of the arcades or the more indolent charms of a deckchair on the seafront. The seaside seems to offer so many different things to us. Even on a cold and blustery winter day any seaside resort will have its promenaders, hardy swimmers and dog exercisers breathing in the fresh air.

In the summertime our resorts are transformed into vibrant and pulsing places, bursting with fun-seekers filling up the attractions, restaurants and shops on offer irrespective of the fickle British weather. Close your eyes, let the sand ooze through your toes and lift your head as the sun peeks through and you could be in Barbados. Ah, if only every day was like that.

Millions of us flock to our seaside resorts every year.

Despite a tough few decades when the sun-warmed hotels of the Mediterranean proved more attractive than a bed and breakfast in Blackpool, our seaside resorts are back. They are regenerating, smartening up, investing in unique Edwardian and Victorian architectural gems and adding new attractions and cultural galleries to a hugely varied selection of historically significant towns and villages. And we are enjoying everything we see.

Before the Covid-19 pandemic, according to the *Coastal Tourism Academy*, our seaside resorts attracted over 21 million overnight visitors and a staggering 169-million-day visits. We are returning to these places post-Covid as our love of the seaside gains momentum. It really does seem that seaside towns and villages are enjoying a moment in the sun.

Our resorts have been here before. Many became immensely popular amongst an affluent health-seeking upper and middle-class who couldn't travel abroad at a time of European war. This popularity received a fresh boost as the working classes got onto the newly constructed railways in huge numbers, taking advantage of easier travel, better wages and increased leisure time.

Today's popularity is driven by what appears to be a judicious mix of fresh local and government inspired investment in attractions and facilities, exciting entrepreneurship, an influx of second-homeownership and holiday letting, a better understanding of what the paying public wants to see and feel from the quality of accommodation and food and inspiring ways to offer a year round service that doesn't rely on the sun. Combine all this with the strong emotional ties this island population has with its coastline and a nostalgia and sentimentality for those innocent family days on the beach and our resorts have a potent offer.

Even media attempts to denigrate some of our less salubrious resorts falter in the face of the whims of the British public. Commentators rather snobbishly put down the charms of places like Blackpool, Cleethorpes and Southport whilst thousands of people not only visit these places, they just keep coming year after year. It seems that our resorts have become an essentially immovable part of British culture.

But it is clear that everything is not running entirely smoothly down by the seaside. Our resorts have to juggle with a conflicting and contrasting set of problems. The pressures of short-term tourism, low wages, social deprivation and worsening health, compounded by the hosting of ageing retirees, bring a string of difficult issues to each resort. There are also complex matters to resolve around coastal erosion, isolation, second homes and housing problems stemming from a change in hotel and bed and breakfast accommodation into flats and cheaper lets.

The response to these issues has been the subject of many academic, governmental, privately-inspired and local analyses. Common themes and common solutions keep popping up. The need for long-term investment, re-balancing the local economy, inspiration and entrepreneurship and the perennial search for distinctiveness pepper these national and local responses.

The question of how each resort marks itself out as different to all the others has been key to their development over the last two hundred years. The search for exclusivity and the cultivation of the affluent often contrasted with resorts that proffered a more working-class offer. This distinctiveness continues today, driven by history, geography, entrepreneurship, local land ownership, character and political direction. As a result, we have around our shores perhaps the most fascinating collection of seaside resorts in the world. All worthy of a visit. But where to start? We need a guide.

Bottom to top

Every year the well-known and nationally acclaimed *Which?* magazine publishes a list of over 100 United Kingdom seaside resorts and ranks them 'best' to 'worst'. As the main UK brand promoting informed customer choice, *Which?* is an acknowledged leader in testing products and services. Its publisher is the national Consumers Association and it has over half a million subscribers to its magazine. Consequently a *Which?* report does tend to generate a lot of interest for a variety of reasons.

The 2020 *Which?* ranking stirred up the usual mix of smug smiles, tut-tutting, knowing nods and outright disbelief as each town or village discovered where the 4,000 polled *Which?* readers had placed their resort. With scores awarded for the readers perceived quality of the beach, seafront, food and drink offers, attractions, scenery, shopping, peace and quiet, and value for money, the final ranking put St Mawes in Cornwall at the top.

At the bottom sat Skegness in Lincolnshire, supposedly with half the score of top-scoring St Mawes. Two very different resorts with completely different histories, geographies, styles, attractions and probably, visitors. Perhaps the only thing they have in common is the sea.

So, there it is… the perfect guide to a tour of our English seaside resorts. Time to start at the bottom for a change and trot off to Skegness. Could it really be the worst resort in the country? Was St Mawes truly the best? I would take the 2020 *Which?* list and hop through it, visiting a range of resorts (to ensure a wide variety of different places) working my way up to the supposed jewel in the crown, St Mawes. I would write up a little of the history of each place, set out some of my own musings on what I had found and gather insights and reflections from local people. If Skegness was the worst, how would other resorts compare?

I started to research a list of towns and villages, guided by the *Which?* report. It was clear an introductory chapter would help. Just what had happened in the past to encourage so many resorts to develop in such a short period of time? Equally valuable would be a discussion on what was going on right now by the seaside. Are these resorts in decline, suffering from the departure of sun-hungry visitors jumping onto aeroplanes to Spain? Or are they rejuvenating and regenerating, driven by entrepreneurial ideas and new cultural and educational projects, powered by an influx of new money that is changing the very nature of seaside resorts?

Big questions and no doubt there will be a lot of different answers. It is perhaps too simple to assume our seaside resorts are alike and share common problems. History and geography set each resort's context in place. The type of visitor each town or village attracted influenced the early development and popularity of each place. From fresh air and sea water-hunting royalty to working class families looking for cheap fun and amusements for idle children, each resort developed in its own way to cater for the clientele it sought.

How to get a resort on the map

Of course, the one common feature shared by all our resorts is the sea and we have a lot of it in the United Kingdom: nearly 13,000 kilometres of coast. But the sea wasn't always seen as a popular place to live or visit. Even the people who relied on the water for a living often built their homes, villages and towns away from the ravages of our storm-tossed sea. It wasn't the done thing to build one's home looking out across the water; rather it was a better idea to keep a safe distance away from a port or harbour, sheltered from floods or storms.

Indeed, the whole idea of using the sea for anything other than fishing or as a means of transport took up to the eighteenth century to gain any sort of grip. As the author Travis Elborough explains, the sea was essentially prized for the most part as a kind of 'vast moat, protecting Fortress Britain's green and pleasant land'. What led to this change of mind about the sea was the increasing concern about health. City and town dwellers, particularly those with money, began to seek out ways to improve their health and well-being. Several persuasive writers and physicians of the day promoted the sea and the sea air as a cure.

The word resort comes from the Old French *resortir* meaning 'to turn to for assistance' and the naming of seaside places as resorts flowed quickly from the earliest visitors turning to the sea for healthy help. The proponents of the benefits of the sea and seawater in particular, date back to the late seventeenth and early eighteenth centuries. Following on from the success of spas like Bath, Buxton, Harrogate and Cheltenham, advocates of seawater as a cure-all began to push their theories amongst the monied classes.

Scarborough lays a claim to be the first UK seaside resort, probably as a result of the tapping of a judicious mix of acidic spa water found running down the cliff, with the seaside location. Effectively it was a spa by the sea. A Dr Wittie wrote about the water's curative qualities in the 1660s and promoted Scarborough as a place for healthy life.

The search for cures for afflictions such as gout, which was common amongst the wealthy of the time, but poorly understood and often incompetently dealt with, saw the easily persuadable and gullible well-off begin a march to the seaside. A London doctor, Richard Russell, was a key instigator and influencer in the 1750s. He moved to Brighthelmstone, today's Brighton, then a small and unremarkable fishing village. He published his dissertation on the success of seawater as a panacea for all ills. Drinking it and bathing in it seemed to do the trick. Chamekh reports that Russell recommended 'half a pint of sea water every morning at five of the clock' and cold bathing was a prerequisite for 'a great quiet of body and mind'. Whatever followed it was enough to see a surge in development in Brighthelmstone and by the 1770s, a sickly Duke of Gloucester, King George III's brother, was visiting to take the cure.

He was quickly followed by a bunch of Dukes who had their own houses in what was now more generally called Brighton and by the 1780s the King himself was visiting. Other seaside towns began to attract royalty and the gentry, keen to be seen taking the cures on offer. Weymouth, Sidmouth, Southend and Worthing all benefitted from royal visits and King George's own physician commented that the sea air of Exmouth was as pure as that of the south of France. These well-off visitors were not just interested in the waters or cure-alls, however. It was important to be seen in the right places with the right people.

The Napoleonic Wars up to 1815 curtailed travel abroad for the gentry, further guiding the well-off and leisure-rich to these new and 'healthy' resorts closer to home. This growth was promoted by several wealthy landowners who used their land by some sleepy coastal villages as an opportunity to develop resorts for these new visitors. Skegness, Hunstanton, Bournemouth, Southport, Saltburn and St Leonards near Hastings, all benefitted from entrepreneurial landowners willing to take a risk to entice the well-off to their resorts. Not all were successful, however. Plans for Withernsea in Yorkshire never took off. Ravenscar, further up the coast, was doomed by the absentee developer's failure to get things done on time whilst trying to build a new resort high above a tiny beach on the edge of the North York Moors. Not the most clement of situations for the well-to-do.

Here come the hoi polloi

A fundamental shift in the nature and use of these seaside resorts began to take place in the early 1800s with the increasing industrialisation of the country. These changes were led by a number of factors: the arrival of the railway to many seaside towns, the growth of an industrial working-class keen to find an escape from their grimy heartlands, the gradual birth of a 'holiday industry', utilising newly acquired days off and the development of the resorts themselves to cater for a different and more family orientated clientele.

From the 1830s to the 1870s seaside resorts became more accessible to the working classes through the growth and spread of the railway. Coupled with increasing industrial affluence these new workers were gradually granted time off as owners and politicians accepted that all work and no play made Jack an increasingly very tired boy.

The Factory Act of 1850 allowing Saturday afternoons off for millworkers and the 1871 Bank Holiday Act, gave people the opportunity for more leisure time. In the north the practice of 'Wakes weeks' (when mills closed for a week for maintenance) added to this. With increasing accessibility, resorts within a short train ride became the focus of the working masses anxious to access the fresh sea air and entertainments increasingly on offer at the seaside.

Quiet and scruffy villages, where most of the inhabitants relied on the fishing industry, began to grow rapidly as hotels, piers, assembly halls, entertainments and holiday attractions poured in. The railway arrived in Brighton in 1841 and within ten years the population had risen from an already royalty boosted 46,000 to 65,000. By 1850, 73,000 people came to Brighton by train in just one week. Blackpool, today's most visited resort, had just 500 people in 1801 and 2,500 in 1851. By 1881 and the railways arrival forty years earlier, *English Heritage* reported that the population had grown to 14,000 and by 1879 it was receiving nearly one million visitors each year by train alone. Skegness, now the fourth most visited resort in England, had just 300 people in 1851 before the railway arrived and with it a substantial plan for development by the land-owning Earl of Scarbrough. Local historian Winston Kime reported that an 1882 Bank holiday brought 20,000 people into the town.

New hotels sprang up to cater for visitors. Large and dramatic hotels emerged in once sleepy towns, many of which are still busy today. In 1867 the Imperial in Blackpool was completed and in the same year the Grand Hotel in Scarborough became England's biggest hotel. In 1879 the Great Western opened in Newquay whilst others like the Royal Exeter in Bournemouth took over large family homes built a few decades earlier.

Such was the pace of this growth that by the start of the twentieth century, as John Walton put it, England had 'a system of coastal resorts whose scale and complexity was unmatched anywhere else in the world'. By 1911, according to Walton, 55% of English families were taking day excursions to the seaside and 20% were needing accommodation for longer trips. England and Wales had over one hundred seaside resorts with a population of over 2,000, led by Brighton, Bournemouth, Eastbourne, Blackpool, Southport, Hastings, Southend and Great Yarmouth. Walton also notes how the seaside resort at that time reflected completely the population mix of age, gender, class and ethnicity. Resorts had become true melting pots of society, whilst some made attempts to attract a 'particular' type of visitor.

Despite the wish to set a local social tone in certain resorts, the railway system was in Walton's words, 'a great leveller', ensuring that distance did not overwhelmingly dictate the preferences of city dwellers for their favourite resorts. Rather, he noted that what was to differentiate the coastal towns was 'topography, landownership, local government and entrepreneurial preference'.

With such a varied clientele, the expense of a hotel was too much for many visitors. In response, two new and supremely British offers emerged to cater for the less well-off; the bed and breakfast hotel with the much-mocked landladies and the holiday camp, made famous by Billy Butlin in particular. Butlin himself said that they were established partly as a response to the old-fashioned habit of seaside visitors being evicted from their rooms each day by the aforementioned landladies. John Walton has written well-researched and passionate texts on the British seaside for many years and his particular affection for the landlady is clear in his book on Blackpool landladies.

Billy Butlin didn't share Walton's rosy retrospection. He had noticed that Britain's weather wasn't always a picture of blue sky and hot sun and that ejected visitors were often left to wander a cold and windy seafront. Butlin had the idea of developing the holiday camp beyond the initial trade union or religious affiliations, with attractive chalets and on-camp attractions and entertainments for all that could survive the British weather, at a one-off inclusive price. He also brought in a host of celebrity entertainers and innovative amusements.

Butlins camps expanded quickly, branding themselves as year-round facilities to extend the short holiday season. His first one was in Skegness, opening in 1936. By 1963 Kathryn Ferry reported that Butlins was welcoming one million visitors to eight camps around the UK.

The search for difference in a competitive market

Resorts began to develop several unique attractions not seen anywhere else in the inland towns and cities. The seaside became what Fred Gray called 'another place' with architectural features and buildings not seen elsewhere. Piers, large assembly halls, winter gardens, bandstands and entertainment venues were accompanied by opportunities for tastes imported from metropolitan areas that prospered on the seafront such as fish and chips, ice-creams and candy floss.

Resorts also started to differentiate themselves by trying to set a social tone to attract daily or short-term pleasure seekers or the kind of middle-class visitors who could extend the holiday season. Developing towns like Blackpool, Skegness and Southend began to look and feel different to Torquay, Bournemouth and Eastbourne.

More isolated resorts that had an air of exclusivity, without the older Victorian and Edwardian esplanades and bandstands, became more popular with a certain group of visitors. The bigger towns continued to develop their entertainments and attractions in competition for the more traditional mass-market visitors happy to enjoy the bucket and spade, fish and chips and donkeys on the beach offerings for all the family. Kathryn Ferry commented on the search by seaside towns for new and exciting amusements that could extract pennies from punters. Slot machines in arcades appeared everywhere alongside waxworks and shooting galleries. Excitements like the switchback railway and the mutoscope, a device that, on the turn of a handle flicked pictures past the viewer creating the illusion of movement, drove the search for innovation and difference.

New modernist architecture appeared at the seaside with outdoor lidos, entertainment pavilions, daring apartment blocks and dramatic hotels. Continuing a tradition of creating a different feel to inland towns and cities, from the nineteenth century onwards, architects had sought to build distinctive and specialist designs that attracted visitors and gave each resort a brand of its own. The new seaside architecture boasted sun terraces, communal bathing, holiday camps and chalets. A new 'cult of the sun' as described by Fred Gray, became a dominant force in architecture and seaside activity.

It wasn't just the nature of the seaside architecture that marked out these resorts as different. Visitors found their pleasures in more esoteric delights such as the raunchy postcards of Donald McGill. As a trained graphic artist he produced over 12,000 postcards between 1904 and his death in 1962. Some were regarded as a bit too vulgar and he ran foul of the Obscene Publications Act of 1875. In a trial in 1954 he was fined for his ruder productions and many cards were destroyed as a result. Today he has a museum in his name in Ryde on the Isle of Wight and his naughtiest cards seem rather mild in these less censorious times.

Resorts began to change through growth and especially the movement of retirees. After World War One, many became popular retirement locations with the emergence of initially unplanned, seasonally occupied and 'creatively' designed homes that spread like creeping fungus along the shorelines in places like Jaywick Sands, Mablethorpe, Selsey and Canvey Island. Eventually the speculators began to see money in such developments. So began the emergence of large bungalow suburbs, led by the initially much reviled (by the planners and conservationists at least) Canvey Island, and Peacehaven near Brighton. Canvey Island was to become England's fastest growing seaside resort in the forty years up to 1951. By then, according to Walton, half of the thirty fastest growing seaside resorts had 'bungalow suburbs' attached. The spread of commuter-led development was also a feature of many towns, like Brighton and Southport, that sat within a short distance of major employment centres.

Further growth came from the arrival of static caravans offering a cheap alternative to footloose car-based visitors. Lincolnshire's coast was particularly popular. The 1950s saw over 1,000 new caravan pitches a year appearing along the coastline. By the mid 1960s, nights in caravans equated to those in bed and breakfast accommodation and hotels.

The end of the boom time

The 1950s and 1960s saw seaside resort-visiting hit a peak. The big resorts became the places to see top entertainers like Morecambe and Wise. Between 1957 and 1967 the pair never missed a summer season at the two biggest resorts at the time, Blackpool and Great Yarmouth. Not everyone came to the seaside for simple pleasures however. A new sub-culture of gangs like the smart, scooter-riding Mods and leather-jacketed Rockers, Teddy Boys, Skinheads and Punks started to hang out in towns like Brighton and Clacton. Although often over-hyped by an excitable media, these young tribes did little to persuade families that resorts were safe and welcoming.

With the arrival of the 1970s a cold wind began to blow through seaside resorts. An increasingly prosperous and mobile population began to expect more from holidays than the traditional offerings of the larger resorts or the more staid and unchanging smaller towns that had appealed to the non-family better-off clientele. Now holidaymakers began to look abroad. What growth did occur in these resorts came from retirees and mobile commuters who were less interested in the entertainments, attractions and hotels. Consequently, in some towns, even as populations continued to grow, the seaside-driven economy declined in importance.

In the 1970s cheaper air travel and the tremendous growth in good quality and sun-blessed accommodation around the Mediterranean Sea quickly ate away at the heart of the British seaside resort offer. As one-industry towns they began to suffer a steady decline. At the same time, a period of global economic restructuring hit the country and the seaside towns saw growing unemployment, social problems, outdated infrastructure and redundant spaces. As Kennell indicated in 2010, these changes were not solely to be laid at the doors of holidaymakers fleeing to Majorca. Factors such as the growing liveability of cities, their use for city-breaks and the proliferation of leisure centres and local entertainment meant there was less recourse to the seaside. Equally there was a move from better-off families and couples to 'reclaim' certain popular resorts considered attractive and quaint for second homes and holiday lets, changing the nature of the resort from day trips or hotel breaks to ownership and holiday lets.

The effect of this was dramatic. An English Heritage report in 2007 set out the statistics. In 1968 75% of all holidays in the country were seaside-based. By 1999 it was 44%. In twenty-five years up to 2001, domestic visits to seaside resorts fell by ten million to twenty-two million. The future of Butlins resorts became a key indicator of seaside success or failure. Sold to the Rank organisation in 1972, after peaking at nine camps in the UK, closures and sales followed in the 1980s, reducing the current list to just three.

As time passed the British began to develop a curious love-hate relationship with the seaside resort, simultaneously soaking up the nostalgia of ageing entertainments, candy floss and rock sweets whilst denigrating them for their rain-sodden decline. The media began to build a relentlessly negative narrative around the quality of each resorts offer, sneering at what it saw as limited working-class expectations, the lack of a cultural scene beyond tribute bands and touring comedians and the growing poverty and health problems of an ageing population. John Walton, the seaside historian remarked that resorts 'faced a devastating combination of nostalgia and mockery... resembling 'all our yesterdays' with 'tired and outdated' offers.

To be fair, there had been a bit of criticism around from some commentators way back in the 1930s. J.B. Priestley no less, chose to divide resorts and their patrons into two types in his 1934 travel account *English Journey*. He stated that places like Blackpool were 'vulgar, with passive and listless holiday-makers'. In contrast the picturesque resorts commanded a different clientele, 'cycling and walking and playing games in the sun'.

In the 1980s the criticism stepped up a level. Heavy-hitting authors toured the country's resorts, laying out in stark terms what they found, often in very ungracious tones. Paul Theroux, the great traveller, decided to travel round the coast describing what he saw and heard in *The Kingdom by the Sea* in 1983. He found much to dislike; Margate was 'infested with skinheads', there was 'a whisper of illness around Folkestone', Butlins in Minehead 'was just like Jonestown', Southport 'a cluttered resort without much sea' (the tide was out) Morecambe, 'sedate, dull and unapologetic' and Blackpool 'ugly, with foolish and flimsy buildings'. I could go on. He stayed at a range of cheap bed and breakfast hotels and was obviously poisoned by the English breakfasts. But to be fair, he did like Weymouth, 'grand without being pompous' and Tenby, 'so picturesque it looked like a watercolour of itself'.

It wasn't just the journalists and authors having a go. In the 1980s Professor Richard Butler set out what he saw as a cycle of evolution that explained much of what was going on in these resorts. He identified a six-stage scenario that tourist areas would go through from 'exploration' when small numbers of visitors discover a resort, through to 'involvement', 'development' and 'consolidation' to stage five and 'stagnation', when visitor numbers peak or overload a resort creating social and environmental problems and the resort is no longer fashionable even if it remains popular.

At the sixth stage resorts can go one of two ways. Either into decline or rejuvenation. In the 1980s many seemed to be heading into decline attracting the attention of analysts like Professor Butler and the snarky comments of journalists and commentators. But as time passed our seaside resorts started to attract a very different set of entrepreneurs, investors, artists and residents. Rejuvenation was on the horizon.

A very British renaissance

Amongst the gloom, there were signs that the death of the British seaside resort had been called far too early. Despite the clear and obvious fall from a peak in the early 1970s, for many the seaside economy remained strong and vibrant. A 2010 study by Beatty, Fothergill, Gore and Wilson sought to dispel the negative seaside myths. It pointed to a slow but steady growth in seaside tourism jobs since the 1990s with over 250,000 jobs supported directly.

The past heritage of the unique development of resorts began to be not only noticed, but lauded, following reports like that of *English Heritage* in 2007. The necessary political clout of the *Coastal Communities Alliance*, formed in 2007, saw increased attention paid to resorts. Every think tank, foundation and university began to lever itself into the area with thoughts on how resorts could be turned round, revitalised and regenerated using tools, funding and ideas from an eclectic mix of cheaper property, art and culture, seaside entrepreneurs and government intervention.

Also in 2010, a *Coastal Communities Alliance* report set out to guide resorts through the minefield of options and possibilities available to ensure their success and capture a' new optimism about the future'. What was clear was that resorts were not uniform in their status, appearance, or response to the new tourism climate.

Many resorts began a deliberate and planned focus on regeneration built around a mix of culture, quality of life, location and education. Resorts close to major cities expanded as commuter towns, promoting their accessibility and environmental benefits. Places like Bournemouth, Brighton, Falmouth and Aberystwyth expanded their student offers to draw young people into their towns. The most attractive and picturesque villages and towns were hardly affected at all, continuing their second home growth, boosted by the expansion of up-market hotels and shops and restaurant-based gentrification such as in Padstow in Cornwall.

Culturally based investment became a hot topic in resorts as places like Margate, St Ives, Folkestone and Hastings benefitted from new museums and galleries. Annual festivals grew in size and scope to draw new visitors in, even to hardened 'old-school' resorts like Skegness and Cromer.

Acknowledged style icons like Wayne Hemingway, a Morecambe lad himself, turned their design talents to saving the seaside with fresh ideas to bring in new visitors. By 2015 *Visit Britain* reported that an impressive 39% of all British nightly stays were in seaside resorts and numerous articles were talking up, even over-hyping, the return of the resort. Commentators, once keen to denigrate resorts for their tiredness, unfashionableness and paucity of imagination, now found a new vibrancy in places like Margate, Hastings, Folkestone, Bournemouth, Whitby and Tenby on top of the continued excellence of the posher resorts like St Mawes, Sidmouth and Southwold. In 2021 *The Guardian* reported on a new 'self-belief' in Great Yarmouth, driven in part by a post Covid boom in visitors but also by new investment from the Government and Lottery, alongside a new impetus generating employment in many coastal towns: the construction and maintenance of offshore energy turbines.

The scale of the issues facing many resorts could not be entirely massaged away by cultural development, new students or wealthier visitors driven by an interest in galleries and independent shops. In 2021 the Chief Medical Officer produced a report on health outcomes highlighting the continued issues resorts faced. Today the town of Blackpool has the worst life expectancy in the country. Perhaps it's not surprising when so many resorts have attracted older retirees who get older and sicker. They also have large numbers of crowded flats or multiple-occupied homes reflecting low incomes, deprivation and subsequently, ill health. Resorts can be difficult to access, poorly served by public services and lack diverse employment, all factors in increasing deprivation.

A *Social Market Foundation* report in 2017 had found the same issues with a growing economic gap between coastal communities and non-coastal towns and cities, low pay, high unemployment and low educational achievement. Even the *National Geographic* was at it, pointing out the contrast in 2018 between the art and cultural development of the Thanet towns with the continued deeper poverty of parts of the towns.

Much remains to be done to secure the success of our resorts. Recent years have brought in more visitors, perhaps thanks to COVID-19 as much as the imaginative flair of the country's seaside towns. The resorts are fighting back, that's clear. The offer they make, whether it be through the more traditional attractions, amusements or new restaurants, independent shops, high quality cultural initiatives and clean beaches is as important to the future of the nation's health and enjoyment as much as that of the individual towns.

So how are we doing today? On the up, vibrant and imaginative, or stuck in a staid and old-fashioned rut that's perfect for some, but off-putting to others. Let the *Which?* list of graded seaside resorts in 2020 be our guide. Let's hop through some of the graded 120 resorts and compare and contrast. I will look into the history of each resort and understand how each one ended up with the look and feel it exhibits today. Then I will give you some of my personal perceptions of each place and pick out the curious, the eccentric and the plain odd features that our resorts thrive in producing.

Off we go… to Skegness. It must be first, this time.

CHAPTER TWO

Skegness: the return

*Good family fun if you immerse yourself
in the whole tacky spectacle*

Lonely Planet's view of Skegness, 2011

Putting Skegness at the bottom of the *Which?* 2020 list of 'best' to 'worst' resorts in the country was bound to stir up a range of responses over on the east coast. Skegness didn't take it very well. 'Fury over Which? survey rating Skegness as worst resort in UK' screamed the furious but admittedly parochial *Skegness Standard*. Evidently local people and businesses had 'slammed' the report, pointing to the quality of the beaches, inexpensiveness and wide range of amenities. 'Skegvegas is the best' shrieked *The Lincolnite* in response. The town had attracted visitors from the East Midlands for over one hundred years, so the ranking reverberated across Leicester, Derby and Nottingham as all the local papers picked up on the story. Allegations of snobbishness amongst *Which?* readers abounded, as Skegness fans filled the pages with their own tales of love for the resort.

The story could have ended up as tomorrow's fish and chip paper, ironically for a town full of fish and chips. The trouble is that Skegness has form when it comes to these lists. Rather harshly, in 2017 it appeared in ninth place in a list of the

World's worst holiday destinations, alongside Pyongyang and Mogadishu for goodness' sake. The travel website *Destination Tips* described the town as 'a once quaint seaside town in northern England... it is now a pile of dirt with a run-down amusement park idly resting on the land' Ouch! The mayor took umbrage declaring the comments as offensive and only worthy of contempt.

Things were not a lot better in the *Which?* 2019 ranking. Skegness was the fourth worst resort in the UK. 2020 shoved Skegness to the bottom of the list. Then along came the 2021 *Which?* report on seaside destinations, published in April 2021: at last, a chance for redemption. But no: lo and behold, Skegness was bottom again. It attracted one star for the seafront, attractions, scenery, peace and quiet and value for money. Ouch again. Sadly 2022 brought no relief. The *Which?* report for that year dumped Skegness into bottom place for a third time. A nasty habit had become an annual humiliation.

Even the *Lonely Planet* weighed in, warning in 2011 that 'culture vultures will probably run a mile' whilst offering that Skegness is 'the ABC of seaside resorts, amusements, bingo and candy-floss, accompanied by the constant soundtrack of klaxons, tweets and bells from the abundant slot machines and fairground rides'.

There are of course plenty of other 'top resort' lists around. I searched the internet, keen to find an alternative ranking. I just couldn't find Skegness topping any of them. But then, up popped an auto-retailer, Robins and Day, who had found that Skegness was the best town to visit in the UK *by car* in 2020. Yes, at last. They praised the towns easy-to-navigate town centre and low-cost parking. Skegness breathed a sigh of relief as millions of East Midlanders climbed into their cars to seek out some cheap parking.

So far, so amusing. But I have an ulterior motive for this exposition on the ranking of poor old Skegness. I lived there for ten years, ten formative years up to the age of eleven that shaped my accent and a host of memories. I feel for poor old Skeggy. Memories had faded a bit though. I hadn't been back for over fifty years. My parents had decided to abandon their solidly Lincolnshire backgrounds for the heady heights of Oxfordshire, dragging me and my sister away from our coastal life.

I decided it was time to revisit and see, through my admittedly rather aged rose-tinted glasses, whether my old town could possibly be regarded as the worst resort in the UK.

But… the beach

I had to start in Skegness. Let's put it at the top of the list for once, and not just for the ease of parking. Not so easy actually. Even on a cloudy Saturday in May there were queues of traffic heading into the town. The car parks were filling up fast.

A quick walk down Hoylake Drive was necessary, to see my old house. New doors and windows and a fence separating the adjacent semi-detached house were the only memorable changes. No blue plaque on the house next door though. Sad really, as it was where the great Ray Clemence, the Liverpool, Tottenham Hotspur and England goalkeeper, lived with his family. He was a bit older than me and played for Scunthorpe United at the time but, as a ten-year-old, I can remember taking penalty shots at him as he stood in front of the garages we had at the back of our shared drive. Then Bill Shankly bought him in 1967 and the rest is history.

A sharp turn towards the sea and I was back on the wonderful Blue Flag beach that Skegness is rightly proud of. Sadly, the huge dunes that I remember clambering through and hiding away in, had gone, washed away by the relentless North Sea that carried everything south to the rapidly growing nature reserve at Gibraltar Point. In fact, the continuing erosion of the sand along this shore means that beach replenishment is needed on a regular basis. Sand is dredged up from the seabed onto the shore. This whole area is susceptible to flooding and the beaches are an essential part of the town's protection.

Out at sea was another surprise. Huge wind turbines now stalked the horizon. Unknown in the 1950s and 1960s, these new monsters were now our growing future power source. The wind farm I could see had seventy-five turbines and was just one of four wind farms in place, or planned, off this stretch of coast.

The walk into town managed to serve up a few more memories of my time in Skegness. Walking south along the North Parade I passed the familiar Art Deco lump of the County Hotel, then the weird Suncastle, with its castellated roofline and the string of bed and breakfast hotels with their fiddly adapted frontages screaming for custom. Nothing new there.

But Skegness had changed and it was clear that the town was getting a lot of private and public investment. Unfortunately, not all with a mind to marking Skegness out as an architecturally distinctive resort. A huge new Premier Inn, with the design merit of a second-class out-of-town office block, dominated the seafront. Massive KFC and McDonald chains with their

33

ubiquitous industrial estate design chic, welcomed visitors from morning to night. The covered pier on the land side was its usual gaudy, noisy self, full of busy brightly coloured sweet shops and takeaways. But the amusement rides and slot machines looked new and shiny and popular. Every shop, pub and arcade along the seafront pulsed with people, noise and life. Business seemed to be thriving.

The donkey rides of my childhood were still there, with queues of families plonking little ones on a healthy-looking bunch of animals at £3 a time. This time, at the end of the day, the donkeys were carried away in a huge trailer instead of walking back to their fields, braying loudly as they passed the end of my street.

The town's iconic Embassy Theatre, originally dating from 1926, storm damaged in 1978, rebuilt in 1982 and refurbished again in 2000, was clearly flourishing, with its very own popular brand of tribute acts and travelling shows. To cock a snook at the cultural snobs of *Which?* the Embassy had also been running opera, classical music, ballet and Shakespeare plays and it only closes for brief periods through the year. The old Tower and Esplanade Gardens, dating back to the 1920s and now Grade Two listed for their historical interest, were in fine condition, well-kept and carefully maintained. Recent council-inspired improvements meant that the stroll down to the beach from the iconic Clock Tower had been tastefully paved, with the addition of the kind of curved streetlights you might see on an Ibiza seafront. Ah yes, 'Skegvegas' was back. Was I getting carried away? Of course I was.

A one-star town?

Skegness isn't for everyone, as the *Which?* readers clearly showed. They really disliked the town, giving just one star to the attractions, seafront, food and drink, scenery, shopping and value for money. Just the golden beach managed three stars. To be honest it's difficult to find something to eat that isn't a burger or fish and chips and the whole area around the Clock Tower, where the noise and tackiness hits a peak, really does smell of chips. There also isn't any scenery to speak of, unless you like the ornamental gardens and boating lake. Lincolnshire's coast is as flat as a pancake and there are no blue plaques commemorating the past visits of portly and sickening royalty.

Past visitors to the town have not been particularly kind when putting their thoughts into print. Bill Bryson, generally a lover of all things British, wasn't impressed with the Skegness weather. In his book *The Road to Little Dribbling*, he arrived in the rain, always a bad start in the town and pointedly commented that 'there wasn't much wrong with the town that moving it 800 miles south couldn't fix' and that 'it wasn't in the least bit bracing'. He put the famous Jolly Fisherman logo on the cover of his book but failed to get copyright permission from the Skegness Town Clerk. They could have sued him but chose to let him off.

Paul Theroux in *The Kingdom by the sea* was bitter and scornful. He called Skeggy 'a low, loud, faded seaside resort… utterly joyless… its vulgarity was uninteresting… it was painfully ugly and it made the English seem dangerous'.

The big vote for Brexit in the town and surrounding area brought fresh scorn from the liberal press. *The New European*, perhaps not unexpectedly, published a piece in 2017 entitled 'This is why Skegness is the seaside town Brexit could close down'. A reporter spent a day hunting down Brexit voters, pointing to the reliance on East European workers in the town and at the neighbouring Butlins. *The New European* returned in 2022 to find Brexit positivity was now off-topic, replaced by moans about how Brexit had done nothing for Skegness. Brexit had encouraged East Europeans to leave it seems, to be replaced by an acute labour shortage in agriculture and hospitality. Five years on though, the magazine couldn't resist a few pops at the place, commenting on the number of people on disability scooters and describing it as at 'the end of the line, both literally and metaphorically'.

Basically, as author Candida Lycett Green commented, Skegness is unpretentious and happy-go-lucky. And as Bryson also said in a moment of reflection in his book, 'it was the most traditional of all the seaside resorts he visited'. Skegness offers a vibrant, gaudy and varied family offer for all kinds of people and not just the hoi-polloi from Nottingham. So, ease up *Which?* readers. 2.2 million visitors a year can't be wrong.

Relentless self-improvement

I decided to seek out a different view of the town from someone who has, I accept, a vested interest, the local MP, Matt Warman. He saw two versions of Skegness. The tourist town of loud attractions, fish and chips, buckets and spades and slot machines. The other, the local community, working long hours in the summer and coming together to support each other through the wintertime. An ageing population with consequent health needs and low levels of seasonal income was balanced by a still thriving summer economy that was competitive and diversifying. Matt Warman pointed to the 'relentless self-improvement' of the visitor economy, citing the arrival of private planes at the airfield in the Water and Leisure Park carrying discerning visitors seeking high quality static caravans for a stay in the town, or publicans bringing in a Lamborghini to attract young punters.

The towns visitor economy remains strong. Even today, despite the constant sniping and snobbishness, Skegness is a top four seaside resort in terms of visitor numbers and can attract up to four million visitors a year at the peak of the season. It packs a big punch for a town of only 20,000 permanent residents. People know that it doesn't have the beautiful cliffs and hinterland of many other resorts. It's not genteel or refined. Skegness is all about entertainment. It's loud, brash and in your face.

It's also not afraid to dish it out when it comes to advertising its charms. The East Lindsey council mounted a campaign in 2012 to market the summer events in the resort and chose to do so by comparing Skegness with some rather unflattering pictures of rivals Brighton and Blackpool. A council spokesman told the *BBC* that this was 'just a bit of friendly rivalry'. It got right up the noses of the other resorts who didn't regard it as very friendly and even the mayor of Skegness was unimpressed.

But it's clear that under the surface lurks the usual round of seaside problems; low seasonal incomes, poor quality rented homes, an older population of retirees with growing health problems, a shortage of education offers, a lack of diverse employment and the continuing issues faced by being so isolated by road and rail.

How to design a new seaside resort

The story of how Skegness developed into such a magnet for thousands of holiday-makers is a tale common to many of England's resorts. The slightly off-putting name is said to come from Old Norse, with the 'ness' part from the Norse for nose, so it could have been 'Skeg's nose' at one time. Even today the name Skegness is associated by some with cheapness, slot machines and caravan sites. In 2012, the BBC reported on a tourism expert proposing the town change its name to throw off its old image and re-brand to something that would attract a wealthier market.

Up to 1868 it was a fishing village of around 350 people with much of the land around owned by the Earl of Scarbrough. Early visitors keen to take in the bracing air stayed in local homes and the first hotel emerged in 1770. It's still in the southern part of the town and today it's called the Vine Hotel. By the early 1800s the local family of Alfred Tennyson (well before his Poet Laureate and Lordship days) were staying in the town and he would enjoy long walks through the dunes south to Gibraltar Point.

It was the Earl of Scarbrough who saw the opportunity to develop the village into a resort. Engineers Clarke and Pickwell were engaged to draw up a grid-iron plan in 1868, much of which remains today. The wide and still slightly posh Lumley Avenue, bears the Earl's family name. In 1873 the railway reached Skegness, adding impetus to its development. In 1877 a sea wall was completed and the Grand Parade and Lumley

Road (still the town's main shopping street) laid out.

The popularity of Skegness as place for fresh air and wellness was boosted by a royal physician, Lord Dawson of Penn, who in 1880 recommended the town as 'the healthiest place in Britain'. The influx of new visitors brought in by train, often on Sundays, when the East Midland workers had a day off, was not always well met by the local god-fearing population. Complaints were repeatedly made about the behaviour and sheer presence of so many people on the Sabbath. According to Winston Kime, as early as 1883, a petition was drawn up to persuade the railway companies to end Sunday excursions. All to no avail.

The town's glory was to be the new pier, completed in 1881 and the fourth longest in the UK. It had to be long as the tide goes out a long way here. It proved immensely popular, attracting 20,000 paying visitors one August Bank Holiday in 1882, according to Candida Lycett Green. Breached in 1919 by a schooner, it was then smashed apart by the great storm of 1978. The National Piers Society commented that two sections of pier were washed away leaving the theatre isolated and cut off. Plans to link the remaining sections by monorail and rebuild the theatre fell through due to a lack of funding and in 1985, as the theatre was being dismantled it was overcome by a fire. The pier today is a stunted version of its former self with the focus of activity on the landward side where the amusements, shops and attractions are now housed. I was fascinated to hear though, that the most recent owners were planning to restore it to the past 582 metre length. Perhaps it was a bit of cheap publicity.

Hassall, Jenkins and Butlin. Skegness builds a brand

1908 saw the arrival of the 'Jolly Fisherman' poster designed by John Hassall, along with the much mocked but also much loved 'Skegness is so bracing' strapline. The Jolly Fisherman is still in evidence in the town and heavily promoted, with a statue by the Clock Tower. Michael Parkin in *Beside the Seaside* speculated that it could even be the oldest advert still in regular use. Bracing was just the right word to use for Skegness. Back in the early 1900s it suggested freshness and a healthy virtuous lifestyle. Strangely, until the 1921 Health Resorts and Watering Places Act, municipal authorities were not allowed to spend money on promoting their resorts. They got round this by encouraging others to do so, like the Skegness Advancement Association's publication of the 'Jolly Fisherman'. Today, the word 'bracing' perhaps captures the way in which that dastardly North Sea wind can make your bones ache.

The town's fresh North Sea air and relative cheapness attracted a range of private and Union-owned convalescent homes. Golf courses sprang up to the north and south of the town. A second surge in the town's development came from the 1922 decision of the Earl of Scarbrough to sell the beach and parades on the seafront to the local Council, for the grand sum of £15,750. The local Engineer and Architect, Rowland Jenkins, seized this opportunity to redevelop the whole seafront, adding the Embassy ballroom, bowling greens, the Suncastle scheme and a range of attractions to entice visitors to the town. His tenure from 1912 to his death in 1952 transformed the town and he cleverly used government grants during the depression years to fund the changes as well as bringing in the infrastructure the growing town needed.

A certain Billy Butlin was employed in the town as these changes took place, running a hoopla stall. He progressed to bring in a series of new and exciting family amusements, including the first dodgem cars in the country. Before the Jenkins inspired changes took hold of the town, back in 1927 Butlin was less than impressed by what he found. Elborough quotes Butlin saying that he found a place so small, 'you could stand outside the railway station and see cows grazing in the fields'. He could, however, see the potential of the resort as a base for his first Butlins holiday camp. This opened in 1936 a few miles to the north, where no doubt, the land was, to the business-like Butlin, pretty cheap. Butlin established a very different sort of holiday camp to what had come before. The earliest camps in the town were funded by coal mining unions as convalescent homes. Butlin wanted entertainment and was so appalled to see his visitors moping about he brought in the Redcoats to inspire joy and relentless happiness amongst his guests.

By the start of the Second World War the town was thriving as a seaside resort, known for the beach, amusements and family attractions, all in a carefully nurtured and planned environment by Rowland Jenkins. After the war investment returned to refurbish and renew many of the seafront attractions but all largely sympathetic to the Jenkins plans. The Embassy Ballroom was rebuilt and new attractions like the Aquarium and Seal Sanctuary arrived.

Boomtown to statistically, bottom of the pile

The sixties saw Skegness bulging with holidaymakers on

sunny summer days and weekends. In 1963 the local tourism officer was welcoming twenty trains bringing over 10,000 visitors each day. I can recall Bank Holidays when the town was bursting with Mods and Rockers and coach and train loads of East Midlanders, so much so that my parents kept us off the seafront on those days. Trouble flared up periodically as fights broke out and the whole town became a curious mix of family seaside fun, noise and ice cream with an air of menace from the various tribes looking for more than fish and chips.

One of the country's first black comedians emerged from the town in the 1960s. Charlie Williams played centre-half for the Skegness Town football club and captained the team. After going solo, he carved out a big career at seaside shows and on TV at a time when stand-up comedians began to get a grip on the humour of the nation.

Skegness couldn't escape the downturn all resorts faced in the 1970s and the decades that followed, even though it continued to maintain its status as a much-visited seaside resort and remained popular enough for the attractions and amusements to stay busy during the holiday season. Even the *Connected Coast Board Town Investment Plan* seemed surprised by the continued year on year investment from many local private entrepreneurs alongside the arrival of the big chains like KFC, McDonalds and Premier Inn.

What became clearer however, was the effect on the town of the migration of older and less healthy people, coupled with the low and seasonal incomes of the tourist trade. By 2013 it was being described as the 'most deprived town in the country' and 'abandoned to poverty'. An *Office for National Statistics* report on fifty-seven seaside resorts picked out Skegness, with neighbour Ingoldmells, as the most deprived of the group for a combination of income, health, education, unemployment and crime measures. Seven years later the East Lindsey area of Lincolnshire, in which Skegness sits, had twice the number of over 65's compared to the England average and a substantially lower working population. Skegness also lies in the bottom 10% in terms of skills rankings in the national Indices of Deprivation, leading to an average salary of £100 less than the national weekly figure.

The 2021 Census results showed little improvement. The East Lindsey area continued to have the worst deprivation levels in England and Wales with the Skegness Town ward displaying over 70% of its population in deprivation when considering unemployment, education, health or overcrowding.

With statistics like these it's not surprising that the local attempts to tackle the town's presenting problems have focused on education, skills, health improvement, new local enterprises to support the environment and tourism and overcoming the isolation of Skegness in terms of transport and broadband. Plans for the first full-scale further education hub have now been submitted on the edge of town along with a planned expansion of 1,000 new homes so there is hope that new investment will start to tackle these deep-seated problems.

It's also the case that Skegness is yet another resort chasing the holy grail of year-round tourism. To me, the eight months of the year when wind-whipped Skeggy was only for us hardened locals, were actually the good times. Some of the local rides in the amusement arcade would let us ride for free as they fired up their machines to stop them seizing up. These days the search for year-round attractions has even seen Skegness wander down the culture road with its own *SO* international arts festival. Although badly Covid affected, it has tried to appeal to local people as much as tourists with events throughout the year. Trouble is, as the local MP identified himself, people don't necessarily come to Skeggy for culture, landscape or historical sights. People know what it offers and like it.

Butlins is trying to buck the short season trend and you can book short stays throughout the year. But as the recent government report *The future of seaside towns* discovered, trying to run for a whole year presented a number of challenges, primarily built around the cultural mindset of many young people about hospitality. Low pay, long hours and limited opportunities for progression meant that sourcing staff across the year was problematic. Perversely, in Brexit-voting Skegness, gaps were being filled by East Europeans, perhaps adding to the local perceptions of an East European takeover when put alongside their high rates of employment in the other local unfashionable business, agriculture. To be fair to the local youth, the lack of good further education colleges and long-term apprenticeships narrowed their ability to see an opportunity in management or hospitality. Hence the *Connected Coast* promotion of better education opportunities outside of school.

Time to escape

My return to Skegness had to include a visit to the nature reserve of Gibraltar Point, a short journey south down the coastline to the point where all the sand from the dunes I used to play in has now ended up as a result of coastal erosion. It's another world when compared to the flashy and noisy seafront.

Although it now has a new Information Centre and café it's still a quiet and serene spot cut through by the slow running and boat-laden Steeping River. Another surprise was that over the last fifty years the Nature reserve had massively increased in size. All that sand washing down from the northern beaches had settled at the Point and was now busy creating new salt-marsh. The wading and migrating birds love the area and it's a complete escape from the excitement of the seafront, just a couple of miles away.

As I left Skegness, I mulled over my feelings during the long, very long drive through the flat Fens. I was strangely optimistic. Skegness is what it is. It isn't going to excite the readers of *Which?* because it doesn't have the beauty or genteel charms of other posher resorts. It has always been about family attractions, wild amusement rides, donkeys, buckets and spades, fish and chips and wholehearted fun. Go to Skeggy for that. For something else, go elsewhere.

CHAPTER THREE

Hunstanton: Sunny Hunny, home of tennis and brutalism

*Lee and me were schooled in a tourist town
With less culture than Jeremy Kyle*

From the lyrics of *Hunstanton Pier*
by Deaf Havana who come from Hunstanton

The cliffs were a surprise. I don't know why, but perhaps it was because I expected the flat Norfolk countryside to melt slowly into the Wash in similar fashion to Skegness. Hunstanton has a fine set of coloured cliffs, layered up like a tiramisu. They are not very high, around twenty metres and only extend to the north of the Promenade in Hunstanton for about two kilometres. They bring an attractive distinctiveness to the town, a point not lost on *Which?* readers who gave the local scenery four out of five stars, the highest rating for the resort. For geologists they are fascinating, containing layers of grey chalk, red chalk and carrstone, a sedimentary sandstone much used in the local buildings. They are also in retreat, with coastal erosion wiping away around thirty metres in the last 150 years.

The disappearing coastline is one of the big problems facing several of the country's seaside resorts and in Hunstanton, or

'Sunny Hunny' as it is known, it's a real and pressing issue. It's not just the cliffs under threat. Further south the beach is consistently under attack from the process of longshore drift, zig-zagging sediment south to the Wash. Huge concrete defences and dozens of groynes dot the coastline. Flooding from storm surges has twice in the last seventy years led to loss of life and destroyed property in the town. In 1953 sixty-five people died from flooding.

The end of a long road

Hunstanton's charms as a seaside resort stem in large part from this precarious location. It is the east coast's only west facing resort, offering lovely sunset views across to the distant Lincolnshire horizon. The cliffs and beaches are busy with walkers and families and once you have managed to get to its isolated position on the north Norfolk coast, there are many local attractions within reach including being close neighbours with royalty at Sandringham.

Indeed, the isolation probably accounts for the somewhat sleepy atmosphere. I felt that this was probably caused by the way in which the town had developed and was still being developed. The town's amusement arcades and colourful traditional rides have been corralled into an area along the South beach or cooped up in the weird aircraft hangar by the sea on The Green in the centre of the town. A series of sites were turned over to car parks or fenced off awaiting 'regeneration', of which more later. Some of its own residents have been a bit rude about it too. The band Deaf Havana, formed of local lads, wrote a song called 'Hunstanton Pier' with a lyric that pointedly said that

47

the town had 'less culture than Jeremy Kyle'.

To the north, The Green sloped down to the sea where the carefully tended gardens and broad open grasslands of Cliff Parade separated the eroding cliff from rows of elegant Victorian terraces. Indeed, it is perhaps this sloping Green, with the views to the sea only inhibited by the hanger of amusements on what used to be the end of the pier, combined with the Esplanade gardens and Cliff Parade, that give the resort its distinctiveness. The Green is much used as a focal point for Hunstanton life, hosting shows and a Carnival and is perhaps unique amongst seaside resorts in retaining the original heart of the town.

The town centre dozed in the sun, with a mix of charity shops, cafes and independent shops. The shopping opportunities didn't impress the *Which?* readers who only gave them two out of five stars along with the overall value for money offered by the resort. Out on the edge of town were the ubiquitous and undistinguished huge chain supermarkets with their very different value for money retail experiences.

A man with a vision... and land and money

So far, so unexceptional perhaps. *Which?* readers agreed, awarding it a generally unremarkable set of very average scores. But Hunstanton is a strange one. Perhaps appropriately, its development as a seaside resort was due to the local land-owner Henry Styleman Le Strange of Hunstanton Hall, who saw an opportunity to create an attractive resort on his own land back in the 1840s. Based on similar resort enterprises in Hove, Clacton and Eastbourne, Henry Styleman Le Strange attempted to create a town initially known as 'St Edmunds' and later in 1895, 'New Hunstanton', south of the existing small Hunstanton fishing village.

In 1846 his first building was completed, intended as a hotel to attract the gentry of the time. It was the New Inn, now the Golden Lion and it still stands today. The Green, in front of the hotel, was always intended to be the town's focal point and to add to its impact Le Strange brought the remains of a medieval stone cross from Snettisham, outside the town, to the site, another feature that still sits on the Green.

At first, his venture was not a great success. New Hunstanton was, as it still is today, a long way from anywhere and at that time, miles from any centres of population, along appalling roads. It seemed Le Strange had messed up rather expensively and his hotel became known as 'Le Strange's folly'. Unperturbed he drew up a detailed plan of what his new town was to look like with an 'Old English' style of residential, retail and church buildings, built around the focal point of a typical triangular village green sloping down to the sea.

It was the coming of the railway, as we have found across the country, that really activated the town's growth. With Le Strange at the forefront, a campaign was building to connect Kings Lynn with Hunstanton by rail. Ben Colson quotes the *Times* report of 1856 that 'exertions were being made to… construct a cheap railway at a cost of £80,000'. By 1861 the money had been raised and construction began. Le Strange gave much of his own land for free and attempted to persuade other local landowners of the long-term benefits of giving land up for track and stations.

The Queen's railway gives Hunstanton a boost

Fate lent the new railway a sizeable economic boost when in 1862 Sandringham House, alongside the line, was bought by Queen Victoria for her son, Prince Edward. In 1890 the line was bought by the Great Eastern railway and Wolferton station, by Sandringham, enlarged to handle the influx of royal visitors.

It was whilst the Tsar of Russia was visiting King Edward VII at Sandringham that an apocryphal but highly amusing exchange took place. It is recorded on the Wolferton Royal station website. Evidently the King and the Tsar were out walking, got a little lost, but were delivered to the North Wootton station by a helpful local. On boarding the train for the three-mile journey to Wolferton, the King said to the guard, 'I am the King of England and this is the Tsar of Russia'. 'Glad to meet you' said the guard, 'and I'm the Archbishop of Canterbury… Tickets please'.

Henry Styleman Le Strange died in 1862 just before the line fully opened. His son, Hamon, took on the mantle of growing Hunstanton. Although only a town of around 500 people at that time, because it was now accessible by train, the resort grew and prospered. In 1864 the *Whites Directory* noted that Hunstanton offered '30 commodious lodgings and boarding houses and three first class hotels'. As train traffic increased, the railway company, Great Eastern, built the Sandringham Hotel in 1875. It was to be an opulent statement of intent for the town with its own resident orchestra.

St Edmunds church, Cliff Terrace and the Glebe House School were all built by 1874. Eminent Victorian architects were employed to provide designs for the town's squares and terraces using local carrstone, chalk and flint. The pier was opened in 1870, the Esplanade Gardens laid out by Sandringham's own gardener, male and female bathing machines appeared on the beach and by 1910, according to Ben Colson, four through trains a day were running to Hunstanton from London.

Every resort worth its salt was busy building a pier around this time and the younger Le Strange decided the town needed one too. The pier wasn't a part of Henry's vision for the resort, but his son gave his blessing to a company formed to construct it. Initially it was a working pier, taking cargo from passing ships and only later became a solely pleasure pier.

Famous visitors like P.G. Wodehouse and H.G. Wells were attracted to the town. H.G. Wells proved to be a bit of a naughty boy, provoking a scandal by keeping his mistress in a house in Victoria Avenue. His mistress, Rebecca West had a son in 1913, whilst living there, but was not greatly impressed by the town describing it as, according to the *Eastern Daily Press,* 'the deadliest place on earth'. For Wells it offered a discreet and quiet hideaway. P.G. Wodehouse often visited his friend Charles Le Strange at Hunstanton Hall and used the Norfolk locations in his comic novels.

The period from 1900 to the Second World War saw Hunstanton at its peak attracting visitors and investment. New attractions were added in 1927 with a bathing lagoon and in 1932 the Capital Cinema arrived, now the Princess Theatre. The Searle's caravan park near the South beach opened in 1936 and still dominates the inland area south of the town.

Hunstanton's proud pier end pavilion was burnt to the ground in a catastrophic fire in June 1939. Just two months later Britain was at war and with thoughts and money going elsewhere, the pier end was never to be rebuilt. The pier head and its 800 feet extension into the sea then became the home of a skating rink and a mini-train. The pier extension gradually fell into poor repair and in 1978 a huge storm destroyed what had then become a disused relic. The pier head continued to be used as an amusement arcade. Local people still pine for a 'proper' pier and have never taken the hanger that contains the amusement arcade and bowling alley that blots The Green, to their hearts. The local mayor in 2015 described it to *yourlocalpaper.com* as a 'monstrosity' and the 'wrong building in the wrong place'.

After the war and the deluge

World War Two had a devastating effect on the town with mines laid on the beach and hotels used for troops and evacuees. The Sandringham ceased its use as a hotel, becoming an office base for the evacuated railway company and it continued to be used for offices up to its demolition in 1967. But the town continued to be popular after the war, with up to twenty-two trains a day arriving at peak times with sixty carriages sitting in sidings ready for the return journey.

Sadly, the storms of 1953 caused significant damage to the southern promenade and railway station. Although new sea defences were built the next threat to the town's future came from the closure of the railway station in 1969. It wasn't Beeching (the author and proponent of the efficiency cuts to many of the country's railways) to blame this time. The line continued to profitable and didn't merit his attention and the royal connection probably helped.

In the view of the Hunstanton campaign to reinstate the railway, in 1959 a nationalised British Rail forced the line into a deficit by cutting direct services from London. Further misery followed as cost savings were imposed by removing staff, sidings and one of the lines. A slow death was inevitable as visitors and local use dried up and just before the summer season began in 1969, there was the final indignity of British Rail closing the line for good.

The sense of grief over the closure saw 300 people attend the final train departure. An information board on the site records that a wreath was attached to the last train saying 'Goodbye Hunstanton railway… is this really the end?' The terminus in the town is now a car park and the station site is marked by a tall signal donated by the station at Wolferton, standing forlornly over the tarmac. Two buildings remain, an old coal shed and the refreshment rooms for the station, now the low-slung Waterside restaurant and bar.

The campaign to reinstate the old railway line from Kings Lynn is real and well supported locally. It is being promoted as a way of keeping young people in the town and letting them commute out to Kings Lynn or Cambridge as well as providing better access to the local hospital and the docks in Kings Lynn. Some of the beautiful old stations such as Wolferton and Heacham still remain but are now in private hands, as is much of the line. Some new houses and buildings have been built across it so the chances of a full reinstatement, without some realignment, are slim it seems.

The 1970s brought in an era of unhappy architectural change for a lot of Hunstanton. Many proud turn of the century hotels and homes were demolished in the name of progress but their replacements leave little to admire. Michael Rouse has captured photographs of the many buildings that have disappeared to be replaced by three and four storey apartment blocks with great views but sadly no architectural merit. The Glebe Hotel, the Women's and Men's Convalescent Home, the Country Club, the Addenbrooke's Hospital Home and the huge Sandringham Hotel were all replaced.

A legacy of curiosities

The legacy of Henry Styleman Le Strange can be seen throughout the town in his urban design and use of local materials and buildings as well as the continuing ownership of 6,200 acres of land in the area. There is no doubt that without him and the continuing work of his son, and undoubtedly the arrival of the railway, there would not be the town we see today. To mark his impact, a life-sized statue to Henry was placed on the open green that slopes down to the sea, gazing out across his Promenade.

The history of the creation of the town is, however, just one of several what you might call, curiosities, or perhaps more generously, features of Sunny Hunny. For Hunstanton can boast the second largest tennis tournament in the UK, a listed Brutalist secondary school, Britain's biggest joke shop, (I kid you not), the site of the first landing in the country of our first patron saint, the largest gable wall of carrstone in the world holding up the Princess Theatre and, if local people have their way, it might even see one of the first reinstated railway lines in the country. So much for being sleepy.

Much ado about a landing

To begin at the beginning, we should go back to 855 AD when Edmund, the appointed King of East Anglia, came ashore at Hunstanton from Saxony. He had to do battle with the Vikings who were storming through the area in 869 AD but was captured, tortured and eventually, it is said, his head was chopped off and separated from his body. There is a fable that his head was guarded by a talking wolf who shouted to Edmund's supporters where they could find his head. Edmund was buried in a small town that eventually became Bury St Edmunds and his burial place became an essential pilgrimage spot in the Middle Ages. Although he became the first patron Saint of England, he was usurped centuries later by St George. It is said that he would be a more relevant patron saint than St George, who possibly never even came to England and has claims laid on him from Malta to Montenegro. At least Edmund was English and lived and died here.

Hunstanton has lived long on this legend. It has its own St Edmunds trail and wolf sculpture even though none of the historical action, other than the landing, actually took place near the town. Nevertheless, Edmund's arrival at the shore has sparked the naming of two streets, two churches, a new housing estate and a ruined thirteenth century chapel after him as well as a campaign to rename the town as Hunstanton St Edmunds.

New balls please

How on earth did the locationally challenged and distinctly un-sporty Hunstanton end up hosting the second biggest tennis tournament in the country? Perhaps even the biggest tennis tournament in the country. After all the average age of the town's residents is 59, twenty years more than the national average and 43% of the population of 5,000 is over 65. Perhaps not a natural choice for so athletic a game.

It's a question I put to Chris Holt, the tournaments Secretary for an astonishing 38 years. Chris is Hunstanton through and through; born in Old Hunstanton he remembers the devastation of the 1953 floods and stayed on to become a Science and photography teacher at Smithdon school for 38 years. Clearly now a local legend, he was given an award by the Lawn Tennis Association for his service to tennis in 2020. He pointed to the whole tournament initially coming from the local gin and tonic set back in 1920, meeting up, socialising and enjoying a game of tennis. And year by year it got bigger.

The annual tournament now attracts nearly 1,200 participants on 38 courts, 28 of which must be constructed from scratch by Chris and his volunteers, the week before the competition starts. The whole thing gradually grew from a social club to the wonderfully British and fully amateur show it is today. Past winners included the Wimbledon winner Ann Jones in 1955.

Chris kindly sent me a copy of the tournaments excellent publication celebrating 100 years of tennis in the town. It's called *Wimbledon-on-Sea* of course. It notes a *Daily Telegraph* article from 2004 saying that it 'is organised for love and played for fun'. Mind you the same paper also ran a story that year headed 'Wimbledon-on-Sea braced for the brats'. Occasional anti-social behaviour seems to be a risk to the tournaments success and more trouble flared up in 2022 as youngsters gathered in local villages and beaches. It seems not every young player stuck to the tennis.

Rather strangely, Chris told me there is now no tennis club in Hunstanton. He got tired of opening up the permanent courts for the club and no-one turning up, so the club folded. But Hunstanton still hums with youthful exuberance during the tennis week. It is a fantastic achievement and despite the Covid inspired cancellations for the last two years, has now passed its centenary.

Joking aside…

So, who wouldn't be drawn into a store advertising itself as the 'World's biggest Joke shop'? There it is on the St Edmunds Terrace a block away from the seafront, the 'World of Fun'. I had to visit. Maybe other joke shops are fairly small, but it didn't strike me as huge in size. What was enormous though was the collection of 'jokey' materials. There was stuff everywhere and it would have taken all day to browse through it. There is a special adult section too if that's your thing.

The shop was started by a local businessman in 1978 with his first sales being itching powder, joke sweets and whoopee cushions. He claims to have invented the fart spray, but I didn't hear it in use much in the town. I asked the salesperson what was her biggest seller and she pointed to a barrel full of 'fun caps', tiny little throwaway bangers that explode when they hit the ground. I expect Hunstanton locals hate them.

A Brutal school

Not every town can claim to have a school so different it has been listed for its architecture. The Grade II* listed Smithdon High School, built in 1954, is much loved by the Twentieth Century Society for the style termed *New Brutalism*. Alison and Peter Smithson were only 21 and 26 respectively when they won a competition in 1950 to design a new secondary school. Inspired by the work of Mies van der Rohe, it was cutting edge for its time with a steel frame and exposed plumbing and steel ceilings. It relied upon the use of ready-made prefabricated parts all exposed and on view. Very un-Hunstanton. The fact that such young architects were allowed to build such a radical type of building at the time was astonishing even to the *Architectural Review* who asked architect Philip Johnson to assess it in 1954. He was particularly surprised by the fact that the Smithsons had never even seen any of van der Rohe's work in the flesh, just his design drawings. Reyner Banham, who first used the term *New Brutalism*, commented that 'one can see what Hunstanton is made of and how it works… it appears to be made of glass, brick, steel and concrete and is in fact made of glass, brick, steel and concrete'.

Every building needs looking after though and 67 years on a major programme of rebuilding has been announced for the school. The stark nature of the building had brought some problems, namely noise transmission and the eventual need to reframe all the glass as it didn't take kindly to the temperature changes in the steel carcass. Chris Holt, who taught there for thirty-eight years said it was called the 'greenhouse', hot in summer, freezing in winter. It has also been questioned over whether it is more of an architectural statement than a building that cares for or is kind to its students.

An uncertain future

What of the future for Hunstanton? Like the Smithdon School it is having to face up to the need to rebuild and revive its fortunes whilst continuing the battle against the long-term threat of coastal erosion and flooding. In particular, with an ageing population, poor connectivity and uncertain holiday popularity the good people of Hunstanton are having to think long and hard about what they want their town to look like, feel like and be like. It works to try and fulfil four functions: as a hub for local villages, a seaside resort, a retirement community and as a commuter town for the employment centre of Kings Lynn. It also has a growing number of second homes (around 18%) and new housing developments on its outskirts, both of which, according to the Council's Neighbourhood Plan, are not universally welcome.

The town has several sites in public Council ownership but seems uncertain what to do with them. Recently the Council invited in Wayne Hemingway to work his magic in rethinking the southern part of the seafront as an accompaniment to a 2008 Masterplan for the town. In plain northern terms he described a 'lack of generosity' from the Council over its charging policies (it does seem to charge for everything, even 24/7 car parking for the disabled) and a strange love of car parks. His ideas included a new pagoda and café, street food pop-ups, beach huts large enough to sleep in overnight and resilient sea defences. Hunstanton decided to sleep on his plans it seems; nothing has happened so far.

The town's residents have expressed their views consistently to the local paper, the *Eastern Daily Press,* calling for improved connectivity, dealing with the slow and congested A149 road to the south, before creating any new attractions, as well as continued investment to replenish and protect the beaches. They also recognise the growing age divide in the town and the need to keep young people living, if not working, locally, with affordable homes, better local further education and employment and apprenticeship opportunities. Current jobs revolve around retail, tourism and the building trades and not much else. Even approved schemes with planning consent are struggling for viability. The town centre bus station, library and new homes redevelopment has stalled and was 'under review' in 2022 due to rising costs.

It appears that the real issues for residents are just too big and too expensive to sort out. Meanwhile the Council fusses over what to do with the scruffy Leisure Centre, vacant sites and over large car parks. Perhaps staying sleepy is a strategy for the future.

CHAPTER FOUR

Blakeney and Wells-next-the-Sea: ancient ports to modern picturesque

> *Those days are gone. There sound no more*
> *The capstan song, the welcoming hails*
> *As some stout trader, fraught with bales*
> *From Eastland marts, draws near the shore*
> *For not to Anglian ports today*
> *Turns England with her swollen needs*

From the poem *Blakeney* by Thomas Thomely

We are now getting to the type of resorts the *Which?* readers clearly love. The village of Blakeney on the north Norfolk coast and the larger town of Wells-next-the-Sea, eight miles to the west are both given high scores for several of their seaside features, with Blakeney sixth on the list in 2020. These are two very different seaside resorts to the 'norm' for Norfolk and its larger towns like Cromer, Hunstanton and Great Yarmouth.

What's pretty surprising though is the score the good readers of *Which?* gave Blakeney for its beach; three stars out of five. Perhaps it was a foggy day when they visited or they decided to apply a little artistic license to their scores but hey, where is the beach?

There is no doubt that Blakeney is an attractive, quintessentially twee and popular village with a fascinating history, much of it still on display in its well-kept streets with over 100 listed buildings. But it doesn't have a beach nearby folks. The village is cut off from the North Sea by a huge six-kilometre-long spit of sand and shingle with mudflats, saltmarsh and reclaimed farmland on the north side of the river Glaven. So, you can't actually see the sea, let alone any beaches.

Yachts in the windows

Blakeney sits on the south side of a curve of the tidal river Glaven. It is a small village climbing southwards from the river quay, through a handful of narrow historic streets, up to the huge and dominant church of St Nicholas. You won't find any traditional seaside amusements here. That's not Blakeney's thing. It's more for the casual stroller, the sailor, the salt-marsh and nature reserve walkers and bird-watchers or for an extended lunch. It is also the spot for a bit of riverside crabbing or to book a boat trip to see Blakeney's most famous residents, the common and grey seals on Blakeney Point. There's also Wiveton Hall, a short stroll away, home of the setting for the 2015 TV programme *Normal for Norfolk* with its equally famous eccentric owner, Desmond MacCarthy. But actually, neither Blakeney nor Wells are that normal for Norfolk.

The scenery isn't for everyone either. Nesta Rogers remarked in *Beside the Seaside* that 'some people go melancholy mad after 48 hours amongst the salt flats' and that the North Sea 'can be the colour of porridge, or alternatively, a pensioned-off battleship'.

Whilst the village of Blakeney is small, with a current population of 800, what is clear is that it was obviously built for busier and more prosperous times. Its active quay (for sailing anyway), huge church, ancient Guildhall, old customs house and quayside buildings speak of different and economically busier times. Virtually the whole older core of the village is a Conservation Area, filled with small flint walled terraces fish-boning out from the narrow High Street into short closes or 'lokes' of flower bedecked cottages. It also seems to be compulsory to have a fully rigged mini-yacht in your roadside window just to drum home the sea-faring past of the place.

You get the impression that time moves much more slowly now. Many second homes are empty and quiet for much of the year and its pubs and shops rely on passing tourist trade. Some things take a while to update too. The Kings Arms still proudly displays an Egon Ronay plaque from 1993.

A history of fishing, trade and obstreperousness

For so small a village it has a fascinating history, revolving around international trading, piracy, hard labour and natural change. It's also a village at risk of becoming a second home museum piece and one that is fighting back with a uniquely local housing solution.

The Domesday Book of 1086 has a mention of a mill in the area called Estnuterle and later Snitterley. Peter Brooks' history of Blakeney states that there is some doubt as to whether Snitterley became Blakeney or whether they were two neighbours, but the name Snitterley has been recorded for posterity on a slate plaque in the village park called The Pastures.

In the thirteenth century Henry III awarded the local manor to John de Blakeney, a fish merchant and the name Blakeney first appeared in official documents. The church of St Nicholas dates from this time. It's a huge and impressive building, a clear sign of the settlement's growing importance as a fishing port. As a mark of this, a Friary was established, at the site of what is today, Friary Farm, owned by the National Trust.

By the time of Edward II in the fourteenth century, the King was requesting ships from the port, so boat building became a part of local activity. Fishing also became so important that the local fishermen of all the Norfolk ports were exempted from war service in 1381. At this time Blakeney Point didn't extend as far westwards as it does today, but it offered a safe shelter to the Glaven river as it widened to the sea.

The legal employment was mixed judiciously with illegal piracy and smuggling. Ships that foundered out to sea were plundered and at times attacked, with goods brought back to the port. Such activity carried on well into the seventeenth century when controls were exerted over the lengths of quay that ships could utilise.

The old Guildhall near the quay dates from the fourteenth century when wool and corn exports to Holland and Belgium were thriving. The Guildhall was once a much bigger building of two stories but only its arched undercroft remains. Behind it sits the Mariners Hill, man-made and thought to be, as it is today, a vantage point over the quay. In the fifteenth century the curious extra tower at the end of the St Nicholas church was added. Brooks says this was for aesthetic reasons to contain a staircase over the chancel but eventually it was used as a lighthouse and could be seen for over twenty miles.

Blakeney had competition from the other Glaven river ports of Wiveton and Cley and suffered from being unable to handle larger boats, a fact underlined by the customs house being moved to Cley in 1565. At times the villages combined to use their power to frustrate royal requests that interfered with their trade. These came thick and fast with each new monarch. Most famously it is said that in 1588 they decided to refuse a request to provide ships for the Spanish Armada.

The sixteenth century saw the peak of merchant activity in Blakeney with regular trading over the North Sea and beyond. But problems emerged from the draining of the salt-marsh that began at Blakeney in 1637 by local landowner Sir Henry Calthorpe. His embankments diverted the Glaven and despite local protestations that saw its removal, the damage to the channels led to extensive silting and Wiveton port was doomed. Blakeney port continued to operate but as ships grew larger and new embankments drained more salt-marsh, cutting the tidal scour each day and silting up the channel, the port relied more and more on coastal trade.

By the nineteenth century a fresh approach and more money was needed to deal with the silting channel. A Harbour company was set up to strengthen and widen the Glaven channel, paid for by a tax on tonnage offloaded. Nature was to have its way, however. The draining of the marshes and the new embankments steadily altered the way in the tides scoured the harbours and the ever-changing marine geography tested the local pilots. The combination of the silting and moving channel and the taxing of ships on what had been previously a free harbour led to declining use of the quay, despite by 1863 the first sailing regatta bringing new activity to the port. By the mid-nineteenth century Cley had ceased its use as a port altogether and then in 1889 the last foreign trade ship left Blakeney harbour.

Brooks remarks that at the turn of the nineteenth century a quarter of the village population still relied on the quay for employment. Local coastal ship trade brought coal, cattle food, fertilisers and malt for off-loading. His reported memories are of hard and poorly paid work in the village with horse-drawn carts carrying goods into the county or to the new railway at Holt. Water was drawn from a host of wells and the village only received a piped supply in 1955. Jonathan Hooton reported that Blakeney continued its use as a port through to 1914 when the Harbour Company was wound up and the village's trading use ended when its granaries shut in 1924.

Tourism, second homes and a housing saviour

The charms of the distant and poor village began to become known to a wider clique of visitors once the railway opened travel to the nearby town of Holt. Early intrepid visitors liked the simple life of a local inn or by staying with hospitable fishermen. Brooks comments on a 1907 edition of *Country Life* running an article on Blakeney and its rustic appeal offering 'many cosy lodgings to be had in the many old, grey flint and tiled houses and many a hearty welcome to be received from the rough but hearty people'.

The village had begun a transition from busy port to tourist haven. The last 'dues' were collected from off-loading boats in 1917, the same year that the National Trust acquired the Point as one of the first nature reserves in the country. By 1921 the old Crown and Anchor on the quay was demolished and the Blakeney Hotel took its place. As the granaries closed and local employment dried up, the village went into decline as a place of trade and work, just as its more picturesque and natural seaside charms were being explored.

However, the village was a long way from todays restored and resplendent condition. Absentee landlords and poor owners failed to maintain the flint terraces and many lapsed into a state of near collapse. At first, as was acknowledged by the local people, incoming new second homeowners saved the village from steady decay. And they kept on coming. It was in 1938 that a determined lady called Norah Clogstoun moved into the village and set about trying to do something about the precarious position of many of these rented homes and the steady loss to incomers, squeezing out local people.

Her protestations to local landlords often went unheard so she resolved to take ownership directly of cottages as they became available. With a loan she bought five houses in 1944 and by 1948 Blakeney Neighbourhood Housing Society (BNHS) was set up and fifteen homes were in ownership at an average price of £112 each, reflecting their sale with sitting tenants. The local booklet on the history of the Society reports that not everyone greeted its work with universal acclaim in the 1950s. Many houses remained vacant and unaffordable and there was some resentment over the lack of replacement homes by the Council. By 1951 though, the Society had acquired thirty-six homes, many in the small yards gathered around communal wells off the High Street.

Norah Clogstoun died in 1963 but the BNHS continued its work, adding a bequest of ten homes in 1984. The Society also benefited from bequests of homes as their owners died and fundraising efforts to support repairs and improvements rolled on each year. By 2011 the Society owned one-third of the social housing in the village. In doing so it had not only made a huge impact locally in securing rented homes for local people, but it had also ensured the traditional brick and flint terraces were restored and renovated, enhancing the villages architectural charm. As the Chair of the BNHS said in 2006 in an *Inside Housing* article, 'Half our homes are listed. We have the sense of being part of the history of the village and its social fabric'.

Today the BNHS website reports it has 39 homes in management with four more leased to Broadland Housing Association. They are marked with beautiful plaques and predominantly scattered down the village High Street.

The village now has 43% of it homes owned as second homes or holiday homes (2018 figures from North Norfolk District Council) and an increasingly ageing population reflecting its growing use by the retired. The Blakeney Neighbourhood Plan reported that nearly 40% of the population were over 65, more than twice the national average. The BNHS and remaining council homes are perhaps the last bastion against the village becoming a retirement and second home community. Village homes are unaffordable to young or poorly paid local people. A two bedroomed terraced house was on sale at £925,000 in August 2021, a laughably out-of-reach sum for all but wealthy retirees or second homeowners.

The Neighbourhood Plan reported that in just one-year local house prices increased by 18%. The prospect of any new and affordable rented homes being built on the village outskirts remained slim and always kicked off a lot of local concern over the changing nature of the village or over-development in an Area of Outstanding Natural Beauty.

This imbalance in the local population hasn't stopped the good people of the village from forming a strong community ethic, however. Perhaps the number of retirees in the village has helped. Local societies and groups are numerous and well supported. There is a local historical society with a mine of well sourced and researched information, an amateur dramatic group, a harbour association, a village hall trust and perhaps, rather quirkily, a duck pond society. This last group was formed to reinstate a duck pond lost to flooding in 2013. It sits by the quay at the heart of the village seashore and local volunteers have ensured the health and well-being of over forty pairs of ducks and geese.

Perhaps normal for Norfolk after all.

Sitting on the dock of the bay, watching the tide roll away

Just a few miles west of Blakeney is Wells-next-the-Sea. It's a small town of around 2,200 people that shares many of the issues facing Blakeney; a relatively quick transition from a busy trading port to a popular tourist hub, growing second home ownership and a shortage of affordable homes driving the creation of another local housing solution. Wells also has an interesting and increasingly dominant neighbour, the Holkham estate, a land-owner and employer with considerable power and influence on the town and its future success.

The readers of *Which?* gave Wells five stars for the beach and local scenery and you can see why. Even though the beach is a good mile away from the town, it is renowned as one of Britain's most beautiful stretches of sand with pine tree-fringes and a wacky collection of much photographed multi-coloured beach huts jacked up on stilts. John Osborne found the beach to be such a tranquil and quiet place he called it a secret British seaside. Mind you he was there on a cold and blowy day and not the height of summer.

It's a favourite walk of visitors from the town to the beach and back, where you can admire the curve of the East Fleet inlet dotted with yachts, the views to the old granary and the attractive working fishing boats moored up on the quay.

The quay at Wells has been an essential part of the town's prosperity for seven hundred years. As with Blakeney, the town dates to the Domesday Book and began life as a fishing port. The name stems from the many small natural springs that provided fresh water for the town. By the 1300s it was exporting grain and later, importing coal from the north, in exchange for wheat and malt. In the seventeenth century the Wells Harbour commissioners were established to ensure the repair and preservation of the channels and quay. Still in place today, the Commissioners recently celebrated 350 years of operation. The town's prosperity grew from malt and grain exports and by the eighteenth century it was nationally renowned for its malt products with sixteen working maltings.

The nineteenth century was the town's high point when it became a ship-building port and over 170 wooden shipping vessels were built here. The very first RNLI lifeboat was stationed in Wells in 1869. A memorial in the town marks the loss of eleven of its crew in a terrible storm in 1880. To commemorate the history of the lifeboat being dragged by horses from the quay to the beach, a cast iron skeletal horse was constructed in the inlet in 2018. It stands tall at low tide but at high tide appears to be swimming through the water.

Despite a decline in trade after the arrival of the railway in 1857, the huge granary building on the quayside was built as late as 1903 and right up to the 1980s boats would be double-banked on the quay off-loading fertiliser and animal feed. The granary closed in 1990 and in 1998 it was converted into luxury flats.

Eventually, ships became too large for the quay and harbour but one of the last and oldest sailing ships still afloat, the Albatros built in 1899, is moored up permanently on the quay as a tourist attraction. After being sold on to a local family in 2021, it was enjoying a full renovation when I visited, before a hoped-for return to Wells.

The town is still a busy fishing port with the Wells Guide reporting that it has eleven crabbers and three commercial angling vessels plying their trade. Further north by the mouth of the East Fleet are the maintenance support vessels for the giant wind turbine stations out at sea in the Sheringham Shoal offshore windfarm. The choice of the Port of Wells as the base for this windfarm has given the port a new lease of life and according to the Wells Coastal Community Team, it has driven fresh investment in navigational and recreational facilities.

A thriving town or Chelsea on Sea

Climbing away from the quay is the narrow shop-filled Staithe Street and Maltings Arts centre, a thriving cinema, community centre, cafe and tourist information hub. This street and those that wind from it, up to the Georgian and Victorian splendour of the tree-lined square of the Buttlands, contain many listed homes, pubs and former coaching inns. On the edge of town are the more prosaic attractions of the public sector buildings, the Co-operative superstore and petrol stations.

Wells has the same housing issues as Blakeney. It has many listed flint and brick cottages and larger Victorian and Georgian houses are popular with non-local buyers, retirees and tourist visitors. Over 30% of the population are over 65. 37% of the towns homes are second homes or holiday lets and as a result, since 2001, the resident population has reduced by 12%. This has created a shortage of affordable homes to rent or buy in the town. Small 'renovation projects' are advertised at £450,000 and a flat in the refurbished Granary building on the quay will set you back nearly £900,000. Even beach huts cost an average of £70,000 and you can't even sleep in them.

Local people are aware of the housing squeeze in their town. Inspired by the Blakeney Neighbourhood Housing Society a similar local housing solution emerged in 2006. A group of concerned local people formed a community land trust called *Homes for Wells* to try and tackle the shortage of affordable rented homes and keep local working families in Wells. Local fundraising, Council support and loans have been combined to provide homes for 54 people so far and the Trust has a high profile in the town.

I spoke to one of their Board members, Annie Golding, a young mum and tenant of the Trust and someone who was particularly pleased to benefit from the work of the Trust. Annie told me that of her old secondary school class she was one of only a few still living in the town. Even those who wanted to stay and work in Wells had been forced to rent or buy away from the expensive coast. Annie loved the local community spirit, the rural life and the beach. But she also saw the downside of being a popular tourist haven with parking problems, more holiday homes and a lack of supporting infrastructure as the town grows. She also pointed out to me that second home-owners and holiday lets don't necessarily bring more money into Wells. Instead, there 'seemed to be more Waitrose vans in the streets bringing supplies in from out of town'. But Annie wouldn't want to live anywhere else.

A powerful neighbour

Wells isn't all community spirit, beach-life, picturesque cottages, attractive quayside and ancient streets, however. It manages to build into its tourist offer a carefully disguised pair of amusement arcades, two outstanding and well-known fish and chip shops, its own miniature railway (sadly under threat of closure) and a steam railway, the Wells and Walsingham Light railway. Apart from the superb beach the other major and growing attraction nearby is Holkham Hall and its estate.

Not only does the Holkham estate own the stunning beach north of the town, but it also owns the entire swathe of drained marsh and beach from Burnham to the west and Stiffkey to the east. It has 25,000 acres in ownership (it owns more elsewhere in Norfolk) including the Pinewoods caravan site behind the Holkham beach, a private walled estate and agricultural land all round Wells. Holkham was also responsible for the embankment that channels the East Fleet on its western side, when in

1859, an earthwork reclaimed over 800 hectares of saltmarsh for grazing.

The eighteenth century Holkham Hall and estate are owned by Lord Leicester, Thomas Coke. His family is well known and seemingly, well-liked locally. Known by their first names, they have transformed their estate and land into a successful business turning over £30 million a year, half of which comes from tourism and just a quarter from agriculture, a third of what it used to be just thirty years ago. In the early 1970s the Coke family faced up to a potential future common to many ancient country piles, when punitive death duties led to sales, break-up or demolition. The family grasped the nettle, took on the running of the Pinewoods caravan site and began the process of diversification.

Today, with nearly fifty different businesses, it is the largest employer in north Norfolk with over 500 people and also, the biggest producer of potatoes in the UK. A visit to the Hall is a carefully marshalled event with a mountain of impressive statistics flung out from a staff team that obviously like their job. They are proud of their eco-credentials too, using anaerobic digesters and producing biogas for 2,500 homes. They even give their tree cuttings to the London Zoo giraffes and reuse zebra poo in the walled garden.

The estate is a big landlord too, with twenty-two tenanted farms and almost 300 residential properties in twelve villages, many of which are let to staff or to local families. The estate takes its landlord role seriously and is proud of the renovation and rejuvenation of older cottages with a declared aim, in its *Holkham Gazette,* to 'become the best house builder in the local area'.

Old and unused agricultural buildings have been converted into commercial workshops and one successful operation run by the jeweller Monica Vinader, has a turnover greater than the entire Holkham estate. Out on the beach Holkham has added a £2 million environmentally friendly information centre and café.

All of this is combined with a slick tourist offer that utilises the estates gardens, hall and parkland for daily visits, festivals and events and a smooth public relations operation that publishes a high quality *Holkham Gazette* and website. The estate supports local charities and sponsors events as well as running a charitable foundation to benefit the local area and its activities. It has recently donated £30,000 to Homes for Wells too. There is no doubt that Wells and Holkham co-exist in a mutually beneficial way, drawing tourists in but also attempting to manage the issues that emerge in a consensual way.

Running such a vast operation does have its problems. At times the estate has butted up against that most battle-hardened of groups, the dog-walkers, when controls have been imposed on the use of the beach to protect nesting birds. It's a curiosity in being both a national nature reserve and Site of Special Scientific Interest but also privately owned. Holkham seems to be catching the flak for the potential closure of the miniature railway that runs to the beach too. As it owns the lease, the estate is 'rethinking' the railways future and other options for the one-mile trek from the town. It seems it is now to be replaced by an environmentally friendly electric bus despite a 50,000 strong petition to save the train.

There is also the thorny issue of the nudists on the Holkham beach. After naturists were banned for 'having sex on the beach' the *Eastern Daily Press* reported that the estate relented and allowed the naturists to return but was seeking to employ a warden to 'carry out regular checks and engagement with nudists' to ensure there was no return to the past hanky-panky.

Presumably they would wear a uniform so they would stand out in the crowd, so to speak. Once again, just normal for Norfolk.

CHAPTER FIVE

Cromer: lifeboats, crabs and the end of the pier show

> There was an old person from Cromer
> Who stood on one leg to read Homer
> When he found he grew stiff, he jumped over the cliff
> Which concluded that person from Cromer

Edward Lear

'No place within so short a journey of the metropolis combines in a more marked degree than Cromer the great desideratum of salubrious and invigorating air, with the glorious prospect of the open sea on the one hand and of pleasing undulating well-wooded scenery on the other'. So began *Jarrolds Illustrated Guide to Cromer and Neighbourhood* published in 1897. I'm not sure what constituted a short journey in Victorian times because even now it can take at least half a day to drive through the Norfolk countryside to Cromer and just as long by train. But Cromer has been a magnetic draw for tourists for over 200 years and retains its combination of invigorating air, open sea and undulating well-wooded scenery. There are many other pleasures to enjoy too and all contained in a proper working town that is more than just a seaside resort.

The fact that it is a real working town and not completely

given over to the god of tourism does mean that at times it is a bit shabby-chic, rough round the edges and a mix of the practical, down-to-earth functionality of a town with a population of 8,000 and the faded Victorian grandeur of big hotels, a busy pier and a well-trodden promenade. But all this adds to the charm of Cromer and I must admit, I liked the place. I think Paul Theroux, on his grand tour of the coast, went too far in saying it had an 'atrophied charm' and was 'rather dull'. To me it felt lived in, well-used, much enjoyed and varied in its attractions.

A walk along the cliffs

Walking in from the west along the coast path, the homes of Cromer stand well back away from the cliff edge with the green sward given over to parking by all things motorised. Once you pass the optimistically named 'Blue Sky' café and the bulk of the Cliftonville Hotel, the very epitome of Edwardian Arts and Crafts faded grandeur (I know... I have stayed there), things pick up by the coast with manicured gardens, the sloping walk of the west Promenade and the cliffs with their bagot goats. These animals, up to twenty of them, graze the cliff edges and save the council a fortune in grass-cutting in the summer months. They are so popular they even have their own goat merchandise.

Behind the Cliftonville is the area of West Cliff, a grid pattern of streets built out in the 1880s and 1890s by the Cabbell family who were the wealthy owners of land in the area. Built as lodgings and seafront hotels the development was deliberately constructed to meet the growing demands of tourist visitors after the opening of the railway.

Moving into the town you pass the Morrisons petrol station, an example of Cromer's tourist/working town schizophrenia, and then Number One Cromer, the well-known fish, chips and crab restaurant. This block marks the start of Cromer's old town, a delightful mix of narrow fisherman's alleys and ancient streets crowded around the commanding Hotel de Paris, a Cromer institution sitting high above the wonderful little pier.

Cromer goes up market

The Hotel de Paris was built in 1830 on the site of a demolished house. The name came from its owner, Pierre le Francois, whose family were escapees from the French Revolution, but it was not the grand structure we see today. In the 1890s it was rebuilt and expanded to take over adjacent buildings. At the start of that century Cromer was just a small fishing village of around 700 people and lacked places for the adventurous visitors of the time to stay. Early visitors found little but bracing walks, the sea-air, sea bathing and lodgings in fishermen's cottages. Lobsters and crabs too, as evidenced by Daniel Defoe in a 1724 travelogue of England when his comment on Cromer was 'I know nothing it is famous for (besides it being thus a terror of sailors) except good lobsters'.

As with many incipient resorts of the time, Cromer's popularity was given a boost by a surgeon called Bartell who was keen to promote its bracing benefits in an early guidebook. It clearly worked, as by 1815, Jane Austen was referring to Cromer in her book *Emma* as a place with 'the best of all sea bathing places... with a fine open sea... and very pure air'.

Several new hotels were built, many of which have now been demolished. They include the Grand, (now a ghastly flat-roofed block of flats), the Marlborough (now the Morrisons garage) and the Metropole (now apartments).

The construction of the railway, in 1877, kicked off a further period of growth in Cromer. Before its arrival Cromer had tried to retain a rather selective and fashionable air with a touch of exclusivity. The closeness of Sandringham and the Prince of Wales, later Edward VII, meant that he was a frequent visitor and golfer in the town, adding to the social tone the resort was attempting to set.

Out with the old and in with the masses

The railway changed all this. West Cliff was built out to meet growing demand for places to stay and a new influx of people arrived. Amongst them, in 1883, was the *Daily Telegraph* theatre critic Clement Scott who fell in love with the place. He was particularly struck by the poppies up on the cliffs and dubbed the area 'Poppyland' in a poem that the Victorians lapped up, encouraging a new wave of visitors. A line from his poem became well used in Cromer's advertising; 'where the regal red poppies are born'. In 1885 a young Winston Churchill was less impressed by Cromer saying in his diary 'I am not enjoying myself very much', a quote the town took to in an ironic way. Others that were more complimentary, from Oscar Wilde and John Manning, were inscribed onto the promenade.

The changing nature of Cromer was captured by a quote from *The Argus* in Norwich in 1887 and replayed to the *Eastern Daily Press* by local journalist and author, Keith Skipper. *The*

Argus editorial didn't really welcome the new visitors: 'It is of course, delightful to see the masses enjoying themselves but I cannot help fearing that the Cromer beloved of artists and wearied brain workers is about to be lost to us forever'.

As Cromer grew in popularity the then owner of the Hotel de Paris laid out the iconic pier in 1901 with an open bandstand at the pier end. It was roofed in four years later to create a theatre. Even then as Keith Skipper relays, Lord Hamilton, of the Great Eastern, which had brought this fresh wave to the town, stated at the Pier opening that he hoped Cromer would never become 'a cheap trippers paradise'. Too late it seems. By 1890 the place had got so bad that local people were objecting to men and women sharing the same lengths of beach for bathing. Shocking!

Britain's best-loved pier

Cromer Pier rejoices in possessing the only remaining full season end-of-the-pier show. It is not a long pier, but it is mercifully free of amusement arcades and prides itself on being a past 'pier of the year' and 'best-loved in Britain' as well as being much used in films and TV. The theatre holds 500 seats and offers, in its own words, a mix of 'rib-tickling comedy, show-stopping vocals, mind-blowing speciality acts and an eclectic brand of dance'. Paul Theroux, on his 80s tour, remarked that the show was like 'observing England's secret life- its anxiety in dismal jokes, its sadness in the old songs'. But by the end he had to admit, he enjoyed himself.

The show has been running for over forty years and consistently wins awards with renowned high quality production values. It's a very popular draw for tourists who not only get to enjoy the restaurant and evening fun but also a casual amble along to the theatre and the lifeboat station at the far end of the pier.

The North Sea can be relentless however and the pier has had to withstand storm damage in 1949, 1953, 1976 and 1978. In 1990 the amusement arcade was destroyed and never replaced and in 1993 a rig cut through the pier to separate the theatre and lifeboat station. In 2004 the actor Stephen Fry, who used to be a waiter at the Hotel de Paris, opened a refurbished theatre, but again storms damaged the pier the next year. The town truly values the pier however and come hell or high water, in 2012, £8 million was spent on its improvement.

When the pier was built the extensive promenade was also extended east and west. The whole seafront captured the hearts of *Which?* readers in 2020 with a full five stars and quite rightly so. Readers also loved the scenery, the town's attractions, and the peace and quiet.

The promenade contains today the classic examples of Cromer's shabby-chic and historical sights. The brightly painted Marine Villa and Bath House both remain from the time of the extension with a collection of both old and new property on the cliff above. The Bath House dates from 1830 and did indeed offer indoor seawater bathing.

After the newer surf school and cafes, you reach Rocket House, the RNLI Henry Blogg Museum. Before this is the Gangway, a ramp up into the town laid out with stones with a raised upper edge to help horses pull loads up the cliff. In the past the horses pulled carts of coal and later, bathing machines. Before tourism arrived, the shallow valley where the Gangway sits was the access into the old fishing village, with all the fishing boats laid out beneath it on the beach as they still do today.

Conservation and crabs

This brings us to another of Cromer's key attractions, crabs and lobsters. Fishing from boats was an all-round activity, for crabs and lobsters in the summer, herring in the autumn and cod in the winter. The Cromer crabs became particularly popular in Victorian times and today the boats you see on the beach concentrate on crabs and lobsters. Down on the beach you can still see the fishermen unloading their pots and showing off their catches, if a little grumpily, to strolling tourists.

Cromer owes its excellent crab and lobster catches to a shallow chalk reef offshore, known as the Marle, where the water is clear and the crabs thrive on the reef's bivalves and molluscs. Whilst the crabs are just the same as the UK's brown crabs, *Fishing News* reports that they are thought to be more slow-growing, packing more sweet white meat into their shells. Hence their attraction to cooks and crab lovers.

The local fishermen are proud of operating sustainably, only hand sorting crabs of the right size or without eggs. Once sorted the crabs are taken to be boiled and dressed, often in the seafood shops and restaurants of Cromer. The town used to have a large seafood factory, Youngs, that took a lot of the catch. It closed in 2012, despite a campaign that saw Stephen Fry renew his acquaintance with the town and come out in support. Another local company, Jonas Seafoods, expanded to fill the gap and is now the towns largest producer of crab and lobster.

The quality of the chalk reef off the Norfolk coast has attracted other interests too. In 2016 it was designated as a Marine Conservation Zone, bringing fresh protections and regulations to the local fishermen. Immediately it also raised questions over damage to the chalk reef, despite the fishermen's pleas about local knowledge and sustainable catches. The *Eastern Daily Press* reported in 2021 on the results of a Natural England survey into the effects of crab-potting on the reef. It found that pots damaged the reef and over time could threaten its long-term life. The fishermen of Cromer didn't respond well to these claims as they had long held the belief that their operations were both sustainable and supportive to the health of the reef. Today there is no happy solution in view to these opposing opinions and Cromer's fishermen feel their future is in limbo whilst Natural England decide on their next steps.

A famous son of Cromer

Cromer's most famous crab fisherman is immortalised in his own building, the Henry Blogg RNLI Museum, on the seafront. As well as crab fishing, Henry Blogg rented out deck-chairs on the beach and eventually became the RNLI's most decorated lifeboatman with a collection of awards for gallantry including the George Cross, the British Empire Medal and three gold and four silver RNLI medals. He first stepped on to a lifeboat in 1894 at a time when the vessels were all rowed and nothing like today's modern craft. He served for fifty-three years and was famous for a number of outrageously dangerous rescues, saving 873 lives before retiring in 1947. He had served as a lifeboatman until he was seventy-four, well past today's compulsory retirement date for the RNLI. His past heroics are remembered in the Museum where one of his old lifeboats from the 1940s has been saved.

Cromer is proud of its RNLI past and the lifeboat's role in saving so many lives. The pier forecourt contains a large inset compass with pointers to where twenty-four rescues took place. Each has an uplifted stone as a reminder of the beacons that were lit on the church tower before the lighthouse was built.

Cromer has another famous son who has also made his mark on the town, albeit in a more prosaic way. Sir James Dyson, the 'billionaire inventor' as he is known these days, was born in the town and attended Gresham's school in nearby Holt. He has generously donated huge sums to the school in the past, as thanks for the school keeping him on after his father died early in his life. But he has also been kind to Cromer, as reported by *North Norfolk News* in 2019, most recently donating a sum to help re-provide a Coastwatch station on the cliffs.

Whilst we are discussing famous folk we can't forget Cromer's most recent visitor, the artist Banksy, who kindly left a bit of eccentric crab related art on the east Promenade in the town in the summer of 2021. As ever with Banksy, it also makes a point, highlighting the need for affordable homes on this part of the coast. The council has made the right decision to protect it, so the tourists can enjoy a bit of Banksy artistic polemic.

A slightly older famous resident

Up from the seafront, New Street shows off Cromer's schizophrenia with a mix of gaudy amusement arcades, crab shops and cottages before you get to the narrow old High Street and

Jetty Street and Cromer's array of pubs and coffee shops. The town was bombed during the war, possibly due to its closeness to military installations and the belief that troops were in the town. As a result, some 1960s infill developments have not been kind to the character of the old town, but its street pattern has been retained.

The main shopping street wasn't too well-liked by our guides, the good readers of *Which?* who in 2020 gave the shopping experience just two stars. Perhaps it is because Cromer's shopping offer reflects its working town nature more than a tourist-based one despite an excellent crop of independent cafes and pubs. What is does contain is the town's little museum and the grand parish church of St Peter and St Paul with the highest church tower in Norfolk.

The museum has details of another of Cromer's little treasures, the West Runton elephant. Initially discovered by strolling beach-goers in 1990, subsequent excavations of a bed on the seashore, found the remains of a huge, fossilised elephant standing over four metres tall, the largest animal that ever existed after the dinosaur period. It is the most complete skeleton of its kind to be found in the world today and is approximately 600-700,000 years old. The sheer size of the elephant was brought to life in 2014 when a skeletal replica emerged onto the beach, constructed by two enterprising designers, to worldwide interest. The real remains sit with Norfolk County in special storage, but the Museum has its own dedicated display.

Common Norfolk pressures

You can see that Cromer has a wide variety of diverse offers all wrapped up in a faded splendour amidst a wonderful seaside setting. For every Henry Blogg Museum or independent café there is a decaying park shelter in need of a bit of 'tlc'. Local people understand the role tourism plays here and broadly, embrace it. There have been times when things have gone a bit haywire, however. In August 2017, the town made national headlines for what was reported as an 'invasion' by the traveller community but in the main, tourism is embraced.

For over fifty years, apart from Covid induced cancellations, the town has run a huge Carnival attracting thousands of tourists. There is usually a wonderfully eclectic and thoroughly English raft of events including best dressed waiter races, glamorous grandmother competitions and of course, knobbly knees. All on top of folk festivals, concerts and gigs in Cromer Hall and the variety of the end of the Pier show.

In 2019 the local paper surveyed Cromer residents and found over 80% welcomed tourism and what it brought to the town. Top concerns were the effect second homes were having on the affordability and accessibility of homes as well as issues over unemployment and the seasonality of present employment. These are common problems across the north Norfolk coast, but Cromer remains more affordable than many of the smaller villages and towns like Wells, Burnham Market and Blakeney and still has more employment opportunities outside of the tourism business.

I spoke to Tim Adams, a past Mayor of Cromer and a County Councillor for the town. He agreed that the shortage of affordable homes and growing number of second and holiday homes was his priority. He would love to see the type of local housing initiative displayed by Wells and Blakeney but also made the point that land is scarce and the town is tightly constrained to the east and west in finding new sites. Tim is a founder of Cromer Cares, a local volunteer led group supporting older people and he commented on the growth in older residents moving to the town to retire and then needing increased support many miles away from their family networks. As a result, social care access in the distant location of north Norfolk was a real and present problem. The number of older people in the town hit the headlines in 2022 when the 2021 census results revealed North Norfolk's leading status as the country's 'oldest local authority area' with one in three residents over the age of 65.

Tim had some interesting statistics on the pressures of tourism too, quoting a low figure of just 11% of visitor journeys to the town by train or bus coupled with a year-on-year growth of 16% in waste tonnage from the town's litter bins. So, more road traffic and more rubbish. But Cromer has its successes too. Tim couldn't think of a single shop that was empty and indeed argued for new shops to widen the shopping offer and diversify into more restaurants and variety.

Cromer is thriving in its own slightly tired and shabby way. The pier, promenade, crabs and varied attractions in the green and pleasant land of Norfolk draw the tourists in, even if it is mostly by car. The town just needs some local inspiration to meet its housing and social care pressures coupled with a bit of 'tlc' in its public assets. There is no need for huge regeneration projects or cultural transformation, just a bit of care and attention for what it already has. Good luck Cromer.

CHAPTER SIX

Exmouth: a little bit of everything

Get the seafront done

Local residents cry for action by the council in Exmouth

To Devon and the resort of Exmouth, sitting at the foot of the river Exe with wide expansive views up the boat-filled estuary and out to Dawlish Warren to the west and Orcombe point, the start of the Jurassic coast, to the east. A lovely setting indeed.

What has Exmouth made of it? Well, there seems to be a bit of uncertainty around in my view It's not just me either. *Which?* readers seemed confused by the Exmouth offer with a mixed set of scores. The town can't quite make up its mind whether it wants to be a trendy and right-on home for surfing and paddle boarding millennials, or a sailor's paradise, or a suburban commuter town or a tourist haven for families with a diverse beach, amusements and entertainments offer. Actually, it has got a bit of everything at the moment, but you can't help feeling it really wants to be properly trendy and attract an active and well-paid set of visitors who bring the right social tone to the town to match an exceptional location.

Hey, trendy young people, come here

It has always been a popular place for visitors. This is how the *Guide to Exmouth* described the place back in 1914. 'Exmouth has all the appurtenances and attractions of a pleasant watering place- a busy square, splendid sands, commodious and well-appointed hotels, restaurants, boarding and lodging houses, excellent bathing facilities and everything that the heart of the pleasure-seeker, the tourist, the invalid or the person in search of rest, recreation or leisured ease could demand'. Gushing indeed.

As you walk the two-mile length of the seafront and the curve of the Exe estuary you see all the modern appurtenances and attractions in play. Starting from the east end of the Marine Drive you stroll by the terrific sweep of the beach, the new Lifeboat Station and past the Maer, a nature reserve that pushes the biggest homes and flats away from the coast in favour of skylarks and sea grasses. Then you come to Exmouth's latest attempt at rejuvenating the seafront; the strange wood panelled huts of the 'world-class' Edge water-sports centre and its trendy retail cabins. These sit alongside the bulk of Mickeys restaurant and beneath, a café, Patisserie Glacerie, inspired by the Michelin starred chef Michael Caines. This is the Sideshore on Queens Road. It was nice to see some new investment and the scheme looked pretty popular on a less than sunny day, but I can't really say that the supposedly 'world-class' water-sports centre matched the pre-development hype. Perhaps there is more to come but I had to check back twice just to be sure the few surfboards I saw sitting around actually belonged to a world class water-sports centre.

To be fair to Edge Watersports, its owners, the Bridge family, are local Exmouth folk with many years of kitesurfing experience and they are having a good go at building an attractive brand. They also co-own the magnificent Beach House on a road that climbs up from the beach. It is a huge Arts and Crafts house dating from 1896 and, according to its blue plaque, may be the first example of a butterfly type of design in Europe, with two wings turning in on a central core. It's available as a holiday home.

Ideas and indecision

The new Sideshore development marks the beginning of the town's regeneration of a beachfront area that once held a host of locally loved, if ageing, amusements, fun parks, cafes and putting green. When the Fun Park closed in 2017, after forty years on the site, local people came out to hold a wake to mark its passing. The local council's wish to regenerate and rejuvenate the Queens Road area has since become something of a long-running saga and is in danger of becoming an embarrassment to the town.

Exmouth is seemingly embracing change, if somewhat reluctantly at times and too often fraught with political indecision. The Queens Road area of the seafront is a classic example of this. Back in 2012 the council agreed a Masterplan for the area where the Fun Park and other attractions sat. Delay after delay thwarted any action and the plans for luxury flats, eateries, shops, a cinema, adventure golf and a café, evidently divided opinion in the town. But the delays didn't stop the closure of the locally loved facilities on the site. In 2015 the Carriage

Café (an actual railway carriage), a local institution for over fifty years, left its site, adding to local residents' dissatisfaction with the plans. To add to the local revolt a survey led by a local councillor produced a sweeping vote of no confidence in the proposals with 95% of over 1,000 residents and visitors rejecting the council's ideas.

In 2016 the council parted company with its proposed developers who had themselves sat back amidst the local uncertainty and done nothing to bring the plans forward. In the same year the Jungle Fun attraction closed down and a year later the Fun Park, after forty years of operation, left Exmouth. The low-slung Harbour Café was also due to go the same year but has had a stay of execution. It too looks ready for change. One local called it a '1960s truck-stop'.

There is also a rather sad looking block of amusements with a crazy golf course attached, tucked away behind the Sideshore, looking out of place amidst the sharp rooflines and solar cells of the new buildings. It's clearly awaiting a Fun Park fate, once the full regeneration force is in play.

Only the Sideshore has been completed, pushed through by a private developer, Grenadier, and operated as a non-profit making company that will utilise all profits for the community once the developer is repaid. A worthy and hopefully successful initiative. Meanwhile the Council prevaricates over the rest of its sites.

The need for change was highlighted to the local website DevonLive in 2018 by the Councils Deputy Chief Executive, who said that tourist numbers of 800,000 a year in 2004 had fallen to 500,000, ten years later. The type of visitor was an issue too. A survey in 2015 found that most tourists were older people with 60% aged 45 plus. 78% visited the resort without children and these visitors didn't seem to spend much in the town, in fact considerably less than the average for Devon as a whole. 65% were solely on day visits but many were returnees with 75% having visited before. The resort was in danger of becoming an older person's haven and this was not what the town wanted it seemed.

The desire for fresh ideas and investment led the Council to the door of Wayne Hemingway and his seaside design ideas. Remember him from Hunstanton? He was popping up everywhere as Mr Save our Seaside. His ideas included the Council's much desired new hotel to generate some income, but also play and events spaces requested by local people. Once again, the Council dilly-dallied. No progress was made on his plans and lo and behold, in January 2023 the Council were once again announcing the appointment of new consultants to regenerate the seafront.

Today the Sideshore development and a new road layout are the first signs of change to this important area, but a large section remained undeveloped when I visited, marked out for kids play with sand pits and benches but clearly just a temporary stopgap. This area was heavily promoted by the council for a series of events and trialled uses to ensure it remained busy and attractive to visitors, but no permanent development has yet started.

As a result, not everyone feels that the council can be trusted to create the right new seaside environment at Queens Road. A pressure group called Save Exmouth Seafront was nonplussed in 2018 by the confused plans of the council and unimpressed by the council's purchase of the Ocean centre, the next block you come to when walking into Exmouth. Local cries of 'Get the seafront done' were reported in the local papers voicing the resident's frustrations with the patchiness of the regeneration proposals as well as concerns for what remains of the old seafront buildings like the 'truck-stop' Harbour Café.

A little bit of everything

The purchase of the Ocean centre, a rather bleak and uninspiring block on the seafront, seems to be the latest problem for the council. Many locals regard it as a white elephant, struggling to survive. Advertised as 'Exmouth's number one attraction' (by the Ocean centre) it offers a bowling alley, soft play, an arcade and food options. The council bought it as a revenue earner in 2020 but doubts remain over its future. Perhaps part of the problem is that the Ocean occupies the old site of the much-loved seafront swimming pool, opened in 1932. It became one of the town's key attractions, with regular swimming and diving competitions and even international water polo matches. It closed in 1985 following the opening of the indoor swimming pool and sports centre in the town.

Walking further along the Esplanade the hotch-potch of styles and facilities continues. You reach the Pavilion, with its auditorium for 550 people and a café. It offers a rather typical seaside fare of tribute acts, rude comedians and army bands, perhaps not something for the water-sport's aficionado over at the Sideshore *Which?* readers didn't rate the mix of attractions very highly, marking them down in comparison with the beach and local scenery.

After the Pavilion you come to the Bath House, a pub that is apparently 'home to the big plate special'. It has a more interesting past than present. Back in the 1790s it was indeed a Bath house with hot and cold salt water on offer to cure all manner of ailments.

Past the faux Arts and Crafts styled Premier Inn, the old Exmouth begins to kick in. The curving sweep of Alexandra Terrace leads up to The Beacon, a terrace dating from Georgian times, full of homes once owned by a crowd of notable people. Lady Byron and her daughter Ada came to live in Byron Court on this road in 1823 after Lord Byron deserted them. Ada, through marriage became the Countess of Lovelace and eventually gained fame herself by assisting Charles Babbage with his development of the very first computer.

Further up The Beacon is Nelson House where Lady Nelson, estranged wife to Horatio Nelson, lived between 1803 and 1829. At the top is the Manor Hotel, once the Beacon Hotel and Exmouth's earliest hotel dating back to the 1790s. At the north end of the Beacon is Chapel Hill and the old site of the Exmouth Chronicle where the Delderfield family lived. The two Delderfield sons, Ronald and Eric became famous for their books, with Ronald in particular seeing many of his stories turned into TV adaptations.

From the Docks to the Marina

Many of these buildings date back to the establishment of Exmouth as a seaside resort. Prior to the arrival of the railway in 1861, the town was a small fishing centre with a port that had been used by Sir Walter Raleigh, who was born in East Budleigh nearby. A blue plaque on the Exeter Road in the centre of the town marks where the Exe shore used to lie and a ferry ran to Starcross over the river. Land reclamation has moved the site inland by some four hundred metres.

The end of the eighteenth century saw the arrival of one of Exmouth's, indeed the country's, strangest buildings, A la Ronde, on the edge of town. Built by two wealthy cousins, Mary and Jane Parminter, it has sixteen sides, is 60 feet high and is filled with the evidence of the cousin's travels. It has shell filled rooms, wall hangings, needlework and bird feathers in a rather mad and eclectic collecting style that is utterly unique. The building is now run by the National Trust after being passed down a female only line in the family. The Parminter cousins didn't seem to like men.

Proximity to Exeter meant that the gentry of the city were attracted to the town as early as the mid-eighteenth century. At first it was the apparent healthiness of the place and its sea bathing that brought the wealthy in. As the *Guide to Exmouth* gushed a little later in 1914, sanitary and health issues remained important for the curious visitor; 'visitors to the town, observing the modern houses, the width and cleanliness of the streets and the scrupulous care of the authorities in regard to sanitary matters, will not be surprised to hear... that of 47 leading health resorts, Exmouth stands first in point of healthiness'.

The shallowness of the Exe approach, coupled with Exeter's control of the estuary and docks in the city meant that Exmouth struggled for business and only had a permanent dock built in 1825 with improvements connecting it to the railway forty years later. A thriving community of 125 chalets operated around the dock. Right up to the 1980s the dock continued to take in ships but the twin problems of larger ships being unable to access it and collapsing dock walls led to closure in 1990.

Today it's been completely rebuilt as the Exmouth marina, a 'prestigious' high-rise development of 300 flats around the old dock with shops and restaurants beneath. Whilst it certainly has terrific views out to the sea and estuary, when inside the square of new flats, I found it a bit soulless and no different to a host of similar marinas you find up and down the coast. Once again it seems to be an ill-fitting piece in the jigsaw of Exmouth. A bit of dense urban chic that has crash-landed from Planet Marina.

Names from the past

The eighteenth century saw a lively smuggling operation emerge. According to *Exmouthhistory.co.uk*, local smuggler William Mutter was jailed when he was caught with a cache of brandy by the cliffs near Exmouth. As with many smugglers his story has been heavily romanticised and he even has a hill named after him near Sidmouth. A blue plaque north of the Maer marks an old smugglers route up from the beach to Mutter's old cider shop.

The arrival of the railway not only brought long term residents and tourists but also the end of smuggling. The many men needed to shift heavy smuggled goods found better and legal employment on the railway. There have in fact been three railway stations in the town and a number of lines. In 1861 the line now known as the Avocet line came in from Exeter. In 1903 a second line opened to Budleigh Salterton with a station at Littleham on the edge of Exmouth. A line also extended to the old docks.

One name you will see a lot of in the town is Rolle. John Rolle was an MP, a peer, a plantation owner, a slaver and the largest landowner in Devon with 55,000 acres. He helped to fund the sea wall in the town in 1842 and the building of several homes, a chapel and gardens. The homes he built were not always of the highest standard, however. John Travis reports that in 1850 the Exeter Board of Health castigated the Rolle's for being unconcerned with the 'class or disposition of the houses erected', with the result that the homes 'were of the second or third class'.

This didn't stop his name being given to Rolle College in Exmouth however, when it opened in 1946. It was closed in 2008 to great consternation in the town. 3,000 students and 400 staff were relocated to Plymouth and, according to the local MP, Hugo Swire, the local economy lost £4-5 million. A community benefit company was set up to try and find new investment and eventually the Exeter Royal Academy for Deaf Education moved to the site with part of it now new housing.

Exmouth welcomes 'the masses'

The arrival of the railway changed Exmouth for good. Commuter journeys from Exeter increased and the resort, no longer difficult to access, welcomed the new tourists. Morgan and Pritchard point to the fact that Exmouth was one of the earliest to encourage 'mass tourism', with day-trippers coming in from Exeter. Many municipal financed investments were made into the seafront with gardens, a swimming pool, entertainments and bowling greens.

By the 1920s Exmouth's visitor population was already predominantly working-class day-trippers attracted by an increasingly eclectic collection of council funded or leased entertainments. These included deck-chairs, ice cream vendors, sand artists, photographers and Punch and Judy shows. Morgan and Pritchard reported that crowds of over 20,000 attended municipal led concerts and orchestras generating huge funds for the council.

As tourist numbers increased so did the attractiveness of the town as a place to live. New housing developments spread out from the old core, fuelled by the successful docks, fishing and tourism. Small terraces were built in an area known as the Colony, to the north of the town centre. After the Second World War commuter and retirement expansion really took off with new private and council estates pushing out to the villages of Littleham, Hulham and Brixington. In 120 years, the population of the town grew from 10,400 to today's 36,000.

The nature of the town changed over this period too. It was no longer a self-contained town with stable local employment. It was now a commuter town and retirement centre as well as a seaside resort. The Exmouth Neighbourhood Plan pointed out that 45% of the working population worked in the Exeter area and a growing number of new developments were being proposed by retirement home and care providers.

The town's housing growth has not been matched by its local retail offer, employment opportunities or infrastructure. The privately owned Magnolia shopping centre is outdated and tired, the roads are crowded and inadequate for the traffic volumes and the economic base remains one of low paid seasonal work. Despite this, the town looks affluent and thriving, due in no small part to the better-off retired residents, working commuters and regular day visitors. It's difficult to see how this pattern of development can change as house prices rise, preventing the young and less well-paid from accessing homes and the wonderful natural environment continues to draw in retirees and the footloose better-off.

As with all the seaside towns we are visiting, Exmouth professes to aim high, in pursuit of being a vibrant, friendly, welcoming, clean and safe place in an outstanding natural setting. Oh, and to be a year-round draw, not just a brief stay-cation stopover. At present it seems to have a bit of everything, a pot-pourri of facilities that individually appeal to particular groups of people who don't mix much, the young at the water-sports centre, the sailors in the marina, the cafes and promenade for strollers, the Pavilion for the evening entertainment and the Ocean for the families on a wet day. Knitting all this together into a coherent whole that still makes Exmouth a great place to live and work will be the town's challenge in the future.

CHAPTER SEVEN

Sidmouth and Beer: Devon's finest

Farewell seductive Sidmouth by the sea
Older and more exclusive than Torquay, Sidmouth in Devon
You are the town for me

John Betjeman

Further up the Devon coast we come to two smaller seaside resorts that are very clear about what they want to offer to their visitors, and it doesn't have anything to do with raucous arcades or huge entertainment centres. With past histories built around attracting the right sort of clientele and current policies to ensure the protection of their built heritage and local environment, Sidmouth and Beer stand out as genteel, high quality and refined resorts.

They are very different seaside resorts in many ways. Sidmouth is a town built around a series of royal and well-to-do connections, a heritage of Regency and Victorian buildings and a seafront promenade tightly squeezed between majestic cliffs and gardens. Beer is a small village compressed around a babbling brook that runs down to a shingle beach scattered with fishing boats and café tables. Both give off an air of respectability and seaside conservatism.

Beer: it does have beer

The village of Beer, six miles up the Devon coast from Sidmouth is the smaller place with around 1,300 residents. Even though it is such a small place it has two major tourist attractions on the village edge and is truly popular with coastal walkers, day visitors and those who just come for drinks and food. *Which?* readers loved the place, putting it in their top ten with five stars for scenery, peace and quiet and value for money.

It also seems to have a hyper-active local community, with plenty of societies and groups, a sailing club, a heritage centre, the coast's best positioned allotments with a view, a busy community land trust taking on ownership of sites for community use and new housing, and a historic fishing centre at its heart. A busy and thriving place indeed. The stunning location and setting make it a popular place to live, as well as visit and the challenge the village faces is to handle both its popularity and enjoyable living environment without becoming a Jurassic coast fossil itself.

Much of the village is in a Conservation area and it is surrounded by an Area of Outstanding Natural Beauty as well as Sites of Special Scientific Interest and Special Areas of Conservation. The coastline and cliffs form part of a World Heritage Site. So not only is Beer special but also vulnerable.

A thousand years of history

Beer has been a popular place to live for thousands of years. In Neolithic times, 4,000BC to 2,000BC, it was the quality of the flint in the Cretaceous rocks that drew early man to the valley. In the Iron Age, from 600BC to the time of the Romans, it was the cliff top sites and their position for hillforts that attracted settlers. But it was the Romans that made the earliest and most extensive use of the Cretaceous limestone around Beer. They found the limestone to be soft, easy to carve and creamy white; excellent material for stonemasons. Their early workings of the stone were to lead to the excavation of the Quarry caves which are still in existence and open to visit today. Vast man-made caverns a quarter of a mile deep have been hewn from the rock and the centuries of use have seen the stone used in places like Buckingham Palace and Exeter Cathedral.

The cliffs have contributed to our understanding of space too. Microbes from the Beer cliffs were attached to the International Space Station and survived for over a year and a half. The *BBC* reported in 2010 that the bacteria were 'everyday organisms' that had been exposed to the vacuum, ultraviolet light, cosmic rays and temperature shifts of space. Quite how they survived was the subject of extended study.

According to Arthur Chapple, a Beer historian, the first documented mention of Beer dates to 1005AD and the award of the land by King Ethelred. The name Beer has nothing to do with drinking sadly. It comes from the Old English *beare* or woodland.

By the seventeenth century Beer was a small fishing village, centred on its pebbly beach. When the Black plague arrived, Chapple says that three-quarters of the villagers died and this led to a possibly apocryphal tale becoming a part of Beer's history. It is said that a Spanish ship foundered off the beach and the rescued sailors stayed in Beer, which was short of men, inter-marrying and producing a population that supposedly, to this day, has a darker skin than elsewhere.

Right up to the turn of the twentieth century the village remained a fishing centre with a long main street and small 'courts' of cob and thatch houses off it. Apart from the fishing, the village became famous for two other activities, smuggling and lace.

Fish, lace and smuggling

Many fishing towns and villages had a side-line in smuggling and Beer was no different. What helped the local fisherman with their smuggling was the use of fishing luggers that evolved over time to suit the local conditions: speedy, light-weight, with a simple sail but also capable of being easily rowed. The boats also had to be easily drawn up a shingle beach and quickly pushed out without damage. The fishermen of Beer gained a reputation as tough sailors, a legacy that continued into World War One when the village provided over twenty seasoned seafarers and even today, since 1975, twenty-five Beer residents have sailed or rowed across the Atlantic.

In the eighteenth century a son of Beer, Jack Rattenbury, gave up the fisherman's life for one of riotous adventure. Although much of his life story seems to be based on his own embellished autobiography, he led a life of smuggling, robberies, mad escapes and fluctuating fortunes. As Richard Platt puts it in his book on smugglers, Rattenbury was a self-styled 'swashbuckler' and probably formed the model for many a fictional smuggler of the past.

Whilst the men of Beer fished and smuggled the women

applied themselves to the craft of lace-making. In the main the lace went on to Honiton in Devon for sale, but many village women sold their work more locally to stave off times of a shortage of work and money. Its origins in the village are unclear but, according to *honitonlace.com*, it may be related to the craft spreading from Italy to the country in the sixteenth century. Right up to the 1970s, the Beer village website reports that the making of the lace was taught in the primary school. The craft as a commercial feature has died out now and today it is just a local hobby.

Busy Beer

Today the village of Beer is picturesque and charming, exuding a well-off air with many carefully restored and well-kept houses, bustling pubs, cafes and shops. Down on the beach, cafes have spilled out across the pebbles, either side of the still active fishing boats, nets and lobster pots. Fish can be bought direct from the end of the spillway with everything from crab to plaice, hake, haddock and mackerel available from the fourth-generation owners of Beer Fisheries.

Overlooking the beach is the Fine Foundation centre, run by the voluntary group, Beer Village Heritage. Together with historical photos of Beer, it has tanks of seawater creatures to give children an understanding of the life of rock-pools. Beer Village Heritage is just one example of the many voluntarily led groups that are thriving in today's Beer. In part this may be driven by the high numbers of retired people in the village. Over 40% of the population are over 60 and this figure is rising. The Beer economic plan from 2016 also pointed to a declining population of under 18-year-olds, down from 18% to 15%.

Amongst these active groups is the Beer Community Land Trust (CLT), founded in 2013 specifically to fund and provide affordable housing in the village. The cost and scarcity of housing in the village, driven by the common problems of retirement popularity and second homeownership, prompted local people to act to provide rented and shared equity homes using an innovative combination of loans, grants and donations. Seven homes have already been completed with six more underway.

Despite its size, Beer is also one of 116 Coastal Community Team (CCT) sites across the country. Established by the Government to help seaside resorts with local regeneration and with access to a Coastal Community Fund since 2017, local volunteers have developed a plan to improve many of the villages most important sites for tourism.

The local action has continued through the Beer Parish council who have successfully campaigned for an asset transfer of key sites from the Council. This proactive move will see car parks, gardens, toilets and open sites in the village brought under the Parish council's control. A small move it may seem, but a significant one for such a little place. Together with the Community Land Trust and CCT, it shows a desire for local people to exert some hyper-local control over their future and deal directly with local problems like affordability and the use of sites and buildings on their doorstep.

This type of locally driven response is becoming a common feature of many smaller seaside villages where tourism, affordability and retirement pressures are not being locally addressed to the satisfaction of organised and committed villagers. Beer is a classic example of this trend. We have already seen the hyper-local action on housing in Wells-next-the-sea and Blakeney in Norfolk. Down in Devon the Beer CLT, CCT and asset transfer are taking things further and showing how small-scale local solutions can really make a difference.

Up market with the Royals

Just along the Devon coast from Beer is the second of our pair of rather genteel, select and well-preserved resorts. To Sidmouth with its Regency splendour and elegant promenade sandwiched between the Devon cliffs.

The Tourist and visitors guide to Sidmouth and its neighbourhood of 1845 was not exactly effusive about the town. The opening remarks were 'there are probably few places in the country to which less historical interest attaches than to the neighbourhood of Sidmouth, which is not remarkable for any event ancient or modern'. Pretty strange really, because by this time Sidmouth had already become a popular and attractive place to visit and live. As ever, at the turn of the nineteenth century it was the well-off who made the first moves with word-of-mouth reports of its deep and almost secret valley.

Visits from the Marquess of Bute and the Duke and Duchess of Kent, with an infant Queen Victoria to be, in 1819, gave the tiny resort of under 3,000 people an exclusive air and new homes were rapidly built along the sea-front to the fashion of the day, Regency Gothic. The sea air hadn't proved terribly therapeutic for the duke however, as he died of pneumonia a month into his time in Sidmouth.

Royal connections had begun in back in 1806 when the

Princess of Wales had stayed at Fortfield Terrace and the Prince of Wales who became Edward VII, came to see where his grandfather had died when on a tour in 1856. In 1831, Helene, the sister-in-law of the Russian Tsar, brought an entourage of one hundred people to the town and stayed in Fortfield Terrace. Queen Victoria's third son, Arthur, Duke of Connaught also made several annual visits. On one, he opened the Connaught Gardens in 1934, up on the shoulder of Peak Hill. Herbaceous borders, bulbs, pathways and a bandstand provided a quiet escape for strollers and the place is still a wonderful Grade II listed respite today.

Just the place for those with 'an overwrought intellect'

The influx of well-heeled new residents saw the development of new houses and villas built in the prevailing styles of both Regency Gothic and ornamented thatched houses known as 'cottage ornee'. The excellent history of the town by the amenity group, the Sid Vale Association (SVA), sets out how this architecture of the period has shaped the town with iron balconies, white stucco, gothic trellis, tented canopies and examples of Horace Walpole-esque 'Strawberry Hill Gothic' creations. The Sidmouth Museum, managed by the SVA, contains a wonderful long picture, from 1814, of the entire seafront promenade and its buildings many of which are still there today.

The Sid Vale Association, established in 1846 as the Sidmouth Improvement Committee, was the first amenity society in England. It has retained its aims of preserving the town and its amenities with a sense of civic duty and responsibility. In 2007 it was bequeathed over £2 million by a Devon man,

Keith Owen, who earned a fortune as a banker in Canada. This fund has been managed to produce a yearly income of grants administered by the Association.

The Esplanade along the seafront, protected by a huge sea wall in 1834, became the site of a few grand hotels. The first hotel was the Royal London in Fore Street, now a shop, which held a ball every Wednesday evening. The first purpose-built hotel was the York, begun in 1807, now the Royal York and Faulkner Hotel. It acquired its Royal tag after the Prince of Wales stayed here in 1856. The Belmont, which became a hotel in 1920, has retained its castellated gateway but lost a surrounding wall. The Victoria, built in 1902, was such a popular draw a special train was laid on from London to bring visitors in for the opening. The hotel's popularity never waned and it has hosted the literary greats George Bernard Shaw and John Betjeman. The Regency styled Bedford Hotel has a fascinating history as a Marine Library and Reading Room when it was opened to the public in 1809 and became a fashionable meeting place for summer visitors. It became a hotel in 1865 after being enlarged into adjoining houses. The Hotel Riviera dates from 1820 and was originally a terrace of three storey houses.

Sidmouth became the go-to place for the well-to-do, as Whittaker's remarked in 1845, voicing the words of one Dr Shapter, 'Sidmouth offers to the occasional visitant the usual requisites for a sojourn by the sea, there are hot and cold shower baths and the sea bathing is good, the beach is somewhat stony though not so much as to occasion great inconvenience... it is well adapted for those who have laboured under affections of the liver... and particularly serviceable in those cases of overwrought intellect… in which the undue wear and tear of the mind is followed by a series of anomalous and depressing symptoms…' How could the rich gentry of the time resist?

Dr Shapter was less effusive about the locals; 'Wrestling and dancing are the only amusements which the working people have, the former of these is conducted with much violence and is looked upon with suspicion by the more respectable part of the community'. Not every member of the gentry was so pompous, however. Nigel Hyman, a SVA historian, reported that it was around this time in the mid-nineteenth century that one of the town's richest residents Thomas Fish, living in a huge 'cottage ornee' called The Knowle, opened his grounds every Monday to allow the local hoi-polloi to roam his gardens whilst he watched from a distance.

The resort continued to attract not just affluent visitors but a host of well-known retirees. Sir Norman Lockyer, the astronomer who discovered helium in the sun, built an observatory on the hill above the town. Sir Ambrose Fleming moved to the town and Winston Churchill's scientific adviser, Professor Lindeman, also lived in the town. General Sir John Dunne, the man who brought the Pekinese dog to Britain, lived in Fortfield Terrace. H.G. Wells and Beatrix Potter stayed in the town and used its location for their stories. Other visitors and residents included Jane Austen in 1801, J.R. Tolkien in the 1930s, the poet Elizabeth Barrett Browning in the 1830s and the author R.F. Delderfield in the 1960s. The town is full of the Sid Vale Association's own blue plaques, marking the location of many VIP visitors and residents who came to Sidmouth.

A different kind of resort

The early nineteenth century saw many seaside resorts transformed by the arrival of the railway. Without one until 1874, Sidmouth's growth languished as a resort and John Travis points to the fact that property prices actually fell in the 1840s and 1850s by around 25% due to the lack of a railway. Even its arrival in 1874 failed to have the dynamic effect on Sidmouth that other resorts experienced. The station terminus, a mile from the seafront up a steep gradient, may, in the view of Nigel Hyman, have put off day-trippers. Whatever the effect, Sidmouth barely grew in size and as a result, retained its genteel, old-fashioned and select social tone.

Its relative exclusivity could be seen in the quality of its big hotels. By 1953 the AA Hotels Handbook listed four three-and-four-star hotels: only six towns in Britain had more. Indeed, Sidmouth continues to be a place of refined sophistication, relatively untroubled by an influx of daily visitors, modernity or even the fashionable cultural regeneration of many seaside resorts. But that does not mean that Sidmouth is a forgotten by-water. The stucco glows with pristine white and magnolia colourwash, the older Regency buildings are lovingly preserved and the putting greens are manicured to within an inch of their lives. *Which?* readers loved the peace and quiet, the scenery and the seafront, awarding them all five stars.

The shopping centre remains a quaint mix of the old and new. Long established brands like Fields department store and Potburys, an omnipresent name in the town, now sit cheek by jowl with trendy seaside shops, independent coffee shops and retailers proudly pushing their green sustainability credentials.

Rockfish, the south coast's biggest sign of an up-market restaurant commitment to a town, has proposed moving into a site at the end of the Esplanade too.

The Esplanade is the place for a promenade and everyone in town seems to be strolling with you. It starts at the foot of the cliff where the Sid river joins the sea. Up the river are the Byes, a riverside park lined with expensive homes on one side and small cottages on the other. The shallow Sid river even has a ford to splash through if you feel brave.

In the town you are immediately struck by the absence of noisy amusement arcades, seafront rides and dodgems. This is a place for a quiet stroll free of the traditional raucous seaside arcades and it's this ambience that is a huge attraction to the still well-heeled visitors in the four-star Victoria and Belmont hotels. The promenading can be continued round the red rock cliffs to Jacobs Ladder and its breezy shingle beach.

Not that Sidmouth is always the place for a snooze on the beach, however. Every year since 1955, apart from Covid interruptions, it has a huge Folk Festival attracting thousands of visitors. Something that hasn't always gone down well with the locals. There is also, just outside town, one of the world's most well-funded animal charities, the Donkey Sanctuary. If donkeys are your thing, this huge farm has worked out a host of ways to separate you from your cash in the cause of donkey welfare. It all started in 1969 with the purchase of one donkey by Dr Elisabeth Svendsen. Her work to save maltreated donkeys and mules became an international mission and although she has now passed away her charity has rescued over 20,000 donkeys and now turns over around £50 million a year.

The lifestyle and environment of Sidmouth has attracted

a lot of retired folks. 43% of the towns 13,000 population are over 65, putting it in the top ten of towns in the country with such a high number of older people. Its popularity with older people has created a problem in the town, however. House values are very high as older retirees buy up property and younger less well-off families are priced out.

The knock-on effects across other services are dramatic. I spoke to recently retired GP Mike Slot, a doctor for 36 years in the town. Hands up, I know him well, he is my brother-in-law. Over the years Mike has seen an increase in palliative and hospice care to cater for the population that has consistently been an older one in his time. In keeping with the uniqueness of Sidmouth the town has developed its own specifically Sidmouth based palliative care charity which has benefitted from community bequests and powerful local fundraising.

Sidmouth faces a few other problems too. A beach management plan is needed to protect the crumbling cliffs and shingle beach and protect the sea wall. It has lost the public sector employment hub of East Devon Council which has moved to Honiton and its grand old home, the Knowle, the site of Thomas Fish's huge cottage and gardens, is now a contentious redevelopment site. The town's sewers seem to be under strain too. In 2018 it became the unwelcome host to a huge 64 metre wide 'fatberg' of congealed waste. Cue much newsworthy hilarity about the residents' habits.

Local residents want to see the quality of their local environment preserved whilst facing up to the perennial seaside problems of an ageing population, pressured public services and families and low-income workers squeezed out of available housing. There is no easy solution as usable housing sites are few and far between and the towns popularity with the elderly shows little sign of abating.

Meanwhile Sidmouth dozes on, happy with its genteel and slightly superior tone, as the cliffs slowly crumble into the sea.

CHAPTER EIGHT

Bridlington and Filey: lobsters, Dad's Army and Billy Butlin

Bridlington in winter is a silent place, where cats and landlady's husbands walk gently down the middle of the streets.

T.E. Lawrence writing to Winifred Fontana in 1934

Let's make the leap to Yorkshire and two magnificent sweeps of sandy beach watched over by two very different towns: Bridlington and Filey, both of which developed in very distinct ways on a coast dominated by the earliest resort of Scarborough.

Bridlington is the larger town with around 35,000 people. As a resort it possesses a magnificent beach of gently sloping sand divided in two by a nose of land where the still busy harbour sits. It's a town of contrasts, both in its fortunes and its look and feel. It mixes the rough and smooth; architecture from the 12th century with an Old Town mix of 19th century and earlier buildings pockmarked by undistinguished 1970s monotony and a melting pot of increasing poverty alongside locally inspired regeneration. To accentuate the contrast even further, how many strolling seaside visitors know that Bridlington is the lobster capital of Europe? More of this later.

Best and worst of all worlds

In February 2021 the *Hull and East Yorkshire News* declared that Bridlington had been found to be one of the best places to live in England. A property agency had ranked over 1,200 towns and cities by architectural merit, natural beauty, quality of life and oddly, super-fast broadband and Bridlington appeared in the top 12% and top in East Yorkshire.

Contrast this with the *Yorkshire Post* headline of July 2021 'Bridlington- the popular seaside resort now ranked one of the most deprived in Britain'. Can they both be right? The Office of National Statistics Index of Multiple Deprivation stated that parts of the south of the town were dogged by unemployment, high crime levels and poor education and health. Family homes and once-thriving bed and breakfasts had been turned into cheap flats for sale or rent and drug dealing was on the rise. In September 2022 the *Yorkshire Post* reported that the residents of the North ward of Bridlington lived, on average, for five years longer than those in the South ward. The paper also reported a local Councillor pointing to a steep decline in the town's fortunes with a loss of well-paid employment, low seasonal wages and a lack of aspiration amongst young people. All just a few streets away from the beautiful beach.

On a sunny summer day though, you see little of this deprivation on the seafront. The South beach in particular stretches for miles to the South Shore caravan site and the long promenade is lined by well cared for houses on one side and thronged by strolling families on the other, walking up to the Bridlington Spa, the town's iconic theatre and conference centre. Dating from 1896 it has been much altered over the years. Burnt down in 1906 it was rebuilt in 1907 and then again in 1926. Another fire burnt it down in 1932, rebuilt again and then refurbished in 2008. It's a Bridlington icon that refuses to die.

Walk further north though and you get to see at first hand the town's mix of confused development. Dominating the South Cliff Gardens is the huge mass of Ebor House, a residential block of no merit whatsoever but possessing fabulous views of the coast. To the north of the harbour, you hit a tacky and loud strip of arcades, pubs, eateries and rides that form Bridlington's more raucous heart. This is punctuated by the big curving mass of the Council's newest venture, the Bridlington Leisure Centre, a £20 million punt to revitalise an old decaying swimming pool. Then there is a much more sedate return to the North Parade Promenade and the huge North Beach curving up to Flamborough Head.

The readers of *Which?* found the beaches and scenery to their liking but not much else, marking down the town's food and drink, attractions, peace and quiet and value for money offers. It seems the town hasn't made the best of its natural attractions and it certainly has the feel of a pick n'mix selection of old, new, tacky and sublime stuck onto the sweeping beaches of North Yorkshire.

Two towns become one

The town's odd melange of styles and incongruous seaside elements undoubtedly stem from its stop-start history of growth over the centuries. What we now see as Bridlington was once two towns, Bridlington Old town, a mile from the sea and built around an ancient Priory site and Bridlington

Quay on the coast.

The continuous erosion on the coast has probably removed any Roman settlements that once stood here but there is clear evidence of Roman activity in the Woldgate, a dead straight road heading off to York from the town and these days the focus of one the town's famous sons, David Hockney and many of his most recent artworks. Hockney often visited Bridlington when staying at his mother's house, which he kept on after her death.

Nothing now remains of the ancient Priory that once dominated the early settlement of Bridlington. It was built around 1150 and demolished at the time of the Dissolution of the Monasteries in 1537. Prior to this it was a centre for pilgrimage as the Sumners note, attracting King Henry V who came to give thanks for his victory at Agincourt. What does remain from the demolition is the Bayle Gate, built in 1388, a huge four storey gatehouse that once formed the entrance to the Priory. The current Grade 1 listed Priory Church dates back to the time of the Priory but was rebuilt in 1846.

The Old town, that grew up to the west of the Bayle Gate, has today many seventeenth, eighteenth and nineteenth century buildings built on older foundations. It is in a well-preserved state in the main and its independent and quirky shops were the perfect setting for the town's most famous film set, as the host of the *Dad's Army* movie in 2016. The town was transformed into Walmington-on-Sea over several weeks and there is now of course, a Dad's Army Trail to follow, highlighting the shops and locations used in the film.

Down at Bridlington Quay (or Burlington Key as it was previously known) was the small port, strengthened by stone from the Priory after its demolition. It had been a harbour from the time of the Priory when monks used it for shipping out their wool. Over time it became a centre for corn and malt trading as well as being a place of refuge for ships in storms and away from privateers. At times over 300 ships found safe harbour around the port as storms raged. Parliament gave the port a special status in 1697 to allow town dwellers to tax passing ships, adding to the wealth of the town. In the nineteenth century the two existing piers were built to protect the harbour and fishing replaced the old trading, with Mike Hitches reporting that sixty-four Bridlington based fishing boats operated daily from the port at the start of the twentieth century.

Today it's a lively harbour for sailors, fishermen and one of the town's best kept secrets: the fact that it is Europe's lobster capital with over 300 tonnes of the shellfish landed each year. The town's fishermen adapted to the decline in fish stocks in the 1990s by turning to crab and lobster with great success. Lobsters command the highest average price of all species landed in the UK but 90% of the lobsters caught go to Europe, whilst we in the UK are busy buying Canadian lobster. As a result of the European trade the effects of Brexit raised its ugly head, erecting administrative barriers that led, rather swiftly, as reported by the *Guardian* in 2021, to the closure of the town's only shellfish exporter after 60 years of business. At the same time the *Fishing News* reported on initiatives to both sustain the quality and longevity of the shellfish beds and build tourism around the town as a food centre, with new restaurants utilising the ports shellfish.

Rise and fall and rise again

Tourism in the town was to an extent overshadowed by the growth of Scarborough but the beaches did attract visitors from the late eighteenth century. In fact, the first Assembly Room was built in 1766 to host the visitors and, according to John Heywood, Bridlington's first guidebook appeared in 1805, waxing lyrically on the sea-bathing opportunities. The successful attraction of the Dukes of Leeds and Newcastle boosted the Quay's popularity as the old town was left to its narrow and quirky streets.

In 1846 the railway arrived and the town began its tourism driven growth. I say arrived, but due to objections from old town residents and traders it was laid between the Old town and the Quay, spurring development that led to the two settlements joining together as one.

Heywood reports that the town's first large hotel, the Alexandra, was built in 1866 'in stately remoteness' at the north end of the Promenade. Modernised in 1907 it rebranded itself as a 'Hydro Hotel' and was the leading hotel in the town right through to a disastrous fire in 1975 and its eventual closure and demolition in 1976. It has now been replaced by a set of rather inauspicious brick-built apartments.

The arrival of the Spa in 1896 brought high-class entertainment and a concert hall known as the People's Palace, with both generating a fresh wave of visitors. These included, it is said, at least by the local heritage website, two Hawaiian princes in 1890, who were said to have brought their surfboards and showed their skills for the first time to a no doubt non-plussed watching public.

By the arrival of the twentieth century Heywood reports that Bridlington had over 900 apartments, 5,000 hotel rooms and twelve boarding houses available for visitors. Throughout the twenties and into the thirties the Spa became one of the north's biggest entertainment draws, supported by the musical director Herman Darewski. The council was doing its bit to support the tourist industry, acquiring Sewerby Hall in 1934 (and having it formally opened by aviator Amy Johnson) followed by the Danes Dyke estate and Flamborough Head. Each offered more extensive attractions to draw people to the town and its more rural and coastal walks and parks.

After the Second World War the whole North Yorkshire coast became littered with static and mobile caravan sites often built hard up against the crumbly cliff edges. The use of hotels and more expensive entertainments declined as holidaymakers found cheaper alternatives in caravans and camping sites or took flights and packages abroad. Bridlington suffered as a result. To its credit the council fought back, refurbishing the South Bay promenade, uniting what was once three promenades into one with new facilities and beach huts.

The Spa had, by 2005, fallen into disrepair and after closure for two years, it was refurbished and reopened. The arrival of the new seafront Leisure World and the boost given by the Dad's Army filming also helped to develop a wave of optimism about the future. Regeneration of the public spaces around the Leisure Centre, seafront and a park around the Gypsey Race stream running up from the harbour helped to perk up the local environment.

Not everything went to plan though. A much discussed £65 million marina, flats and conference centre was blocked by the

Government in 2003 after four years of haggling. It divided the local residents as it would have taken out a slice of the South Beach and harbour walls and many considered it dispropor- tionately oversized for such a small resort.

That wasn't to be the end of it, however. Plans from the Council and Bridlington Harbour Commissioners to press on and build a marina rumbled on right through to 2018 when the axe seemed to fall again after an independent study failed to find a way to create a viable large-scale project.

What the marina plans showed however was that the town remained concerned about its long-term future. Its natural benefits were not seen as good enough or grand enough to draw in the increasingly mobile and discerning future punters and the search for a unique and essentially up-market attraction was seen as the key to success. Without the public or private investment needed for such plans, Bridlington's future seems to continue to be as an essentially regionally based family resort where its judicious mix of beaches, environment and attractions like the Spa, are its focus.

Diversifying its offer into opportunities that bring in investment and a wider range of jobs to help with its growing deprivation hot spots is a tough call on the remote Yorkshire coast. Not even being the Lobster Capital of Europe can help if the lobsters are so expensive, the customers still run scared of how on earth you eat them and the local exporter is forced to close because of Brexit. But Bridlington keeps on trying.

Filey: fishing for the gentry

Just a few miles up the coast from Bridlington is Filey, a small resort of around 7,000 people that certainly had never wanted to be like Bridlington or its northern neighbour, Scarborough. Filey still regards itself as different, a bit select, a bit classy, elegant and understated and despite the rather shocking arrival of Butlins in the 1940s, a resort apart from others on the Yorkshire coast. *Which?* readers liked the place, awarding five stars to Filey's seafront, beach and peace and quiet, whilst being less impressed by the attractions and shopping on offer.

The social tone of Filey, as a resort, was set right from the start of its development in the 1830s. There had been a small fishing village here for at least eight centuries before anyone thought of it as a resort and the town's oldest building, St Oswalds Church, dating back to the twelfth century, still contains a host of identifiable graffiti covering four hundred years of history. Indeed fishing, even in its much-emasculated state, is still a beating heart of the local community. Sadly, it may not be for much longer with just four remaining year-round 'cobles' (small flat-bottomed boats) as they are known, fishing for sea trout, salmon and lobster. Twenty years ago, there were fifteen boats but now the current crop of fishermen fear there is no one ready to follow them.

In the 1800s Filey was a much bigger fishing port with more than thirty yawls (larger boats that could still be beached) and seventy cobles. It even exported dried skate wings to Portugal such was its influence and reach. This is even more surprising given that Filey has never had a harbour and its coble landing was only protected with a timber wall in 1871.

An interesting tale revolves around how the once riotous and rough fishermen of the village found God, through a doughty Methodist minister called John Oxtoby. In the 1820s he made it his mission to quell the swearing, drunkenness and heinous crime of fishing on a Sunday, with startling success. Such was the turnaround that the fishermen formed a choir to carry God's word around and it still runs today as the *Filey Fishermen's Choir*. Not so many Methodists or fishermen though. And it is in need of new members as current members age and drop away.

One surprising fact about Filey is that a naval battle, that took place in the bay in 1779, became one of the bloodiest in the American War of Independence. It is described by Michael Fearon in his history of the town. The story is that a Scotsman, John Paul Jones, was commanding the ship *Bonhomme Richard* on behalf of the American colonies, when it engaged a number of British ships. After point blank firing, Jones successfully overcame the British ship *Serapis,* transferred his flag and then watched his own ship sink off Flamborough Head. He was congratulated on his return by George Washington for what the Americans considered a naval victory. The British thought differently, knighting the captain of the *Serapis* for a valiant fight and defending its flotilla of merchant ships.

The battle took place so close to the coast it was watched by hundreds of spectators. Today the final resting place of the *Bonhomme Richard* remains a mystery despite many American inspired searches. The name John Paul Jones is often seen in the Filey area and rather oddly, the bar at the Bay resort is named after him and not the Led Zeppelin guitarist as people of a certain generation might think.

Up until the late eighteenth century the charms of Filey stayed with the villagers but as the gentry and affluent visitors of Scarborough began to seek a quieter life away from the bigger town's more raucous pleasures, Filey's beach began to attract its first tourists. Foord's Hotel opened in 1815 to cater for the early visitors but real change came in the late 1830s when the Birmingham solicitor, John Wilkes Unett bought land looking out over the coast between two shallow ravines and set about planning the Crescent.

Building a New Filey

It was the Crescent, built over the period 1840-53, a beautiful and dignified five-storey terrace of white stucco buildings looking out to the bay that was to transform Filey as a tourist location for the well-to-do. In part it was not just Filey benefiting from the gentry seeking a quieter and more refined stay than Scarborough was offering but also the town's natural charms and sweep of beach. In the centre of the Crescent was what became the Royal Crescent Hotel, which rapidly became the place to be. The Archbishop of York, and the Prime Minister Lord Russell stayed there. Other Crescent properties hosted many royal visitors and well-known characters like the composer Frederick Delius, right through to the early twentieth century, bucking the trend at that time to leave such resorts for the hoi polloi.

That of course, was the trick Filey had managed to pull off. Stay stately, stay up market and keep the right social tone in place without the diversions that attracted the cheaper end of the market. But as a result, there were two Fileys, Old Filey, with the old streets of the fishing village and New Filey, a grid-iron pattern of avenues around the Crescent with the villas and facilities built to cater for the better off tourists.

These included Ackworth House on the seafront, built in grand French Emperor style to house seawater baths and now beautifully restored as apartments and Langford Villa built in 1830, which often provided a summer vacation to the Terry family of Terry's chocolate orange fame. As Fearon puts it, New Filey had established 'a fashionable reputation' as a resort 'free from vulgarity'.

In the 1920s the gardens in front of the Crescent, once solely for the owners and occupiers of the Crescent, high above the seafront promenade, were bought by a local resident and given to the Council for public use. This has secured their future as a superb backdrop to the promenade as well as giving tourists a terrific garden setting in which to admire the Crescent.

Billy Butlin arrives

Filey's dignified and select status seemed assured right up to the 1930s. But one man was to rock the town with a markedly different type of holiday offer. Along came Billy Butlin with plans to develop what he hoped would be his flagship site, just two miles south of the town. Fearon reports that the council took some persuading, initially rejecting his plans as they represented 'a serious detriment to the neighbourhood'. In 1939, after modifications, building commenced, only to be hijacked by the war. The site was taken over and used as RAF Hunmanby. Butlin got the Government to agree to it passing back to him at the end of the War and with the assistance of 400 RAF men, it was reopened in June 1945. Peter Scott quotes the *Filey News* describing the site as 'Yorkshire's new beauty spot'.

By 1947 the camp had its own railway station and, in its heyday, attracted over 11,000 visitors each day on a 400-acre site. It was a huge success and lays claim to Paul McCartney's first public appearance in a talent show with his brother in 1957.

However, in 1983, Filey got another shock. This time it was the decision by Butlin to close the site completely, blaming declining bookings. Over a hundred people lost their jobs and the local council lost an enormous amount of income. A local speculator took the site on and renamed it, but after just six weeks it closed again. Demolition followed and attempts to turn it into a residential site were thwarted by the council. Eventually a viable project was found, turning it into today's huge chalet and holiday village called The Bay. Michael Fearon stated that at the time the sheer size of the holiday village took local residents by surprise.

The coastal holiday camps and holiday lets closest to the shoreline now face a new threat that is nothing to do with economic viability. This time it is the rising sea levels and daily coastal erosion in this part of the country. An Environment Agency report in 2022 found Filey to be fifth on a list of potentially inundated towns over the next twenty years with a likely forty metres of coast lost to the sea. It's already costing £500,000 to shore up one single access road to the south of the town just to 'buy time' in the words of the local Council.

Today there is nothing left of the old Butlins other than the station platform on private land, itself shut down in 1977 as fewer visitors arrived by train. There is one other reminder of Billy Butlin in Filey. It's the last great villa built in the town, known as the White House and once owned by Butlin. It is of striking Art Deco style in a fabulous location looking out over the beach, with the huge Primrose Valley caravan site, itself once a part of the Butlins site, behind it.

Still select and sedate, Filey sleeps on

A stroll through Filey today will confirm to any visitor that Filey is a resort apart from others on this stretch of coast. It retains a genteel and discerning air with well-kept public gardens and a lovely promenade with just the occasional nod to tourist whims through the Funland amusement arcades on the still busy coble landing. There is nothing raucous or noisy down here at the town's only amusement hotspot either. When I was there it was just two policemen eating ice-creams with a few salty old sea-dogs amongst the lobster pots whilst families dug sandcastles at the end of the coble landing. The town does pay homage to its fishing past with a slightly scary giant lobster on the promenade and another giant, a twelve-foot-tall steel fisherman called Finlay, donated by a Filey lover.

At the south end of the promenade there is still a shallow paddling pool with a superb view of the bay, before the beach road curves up to the low cliff top where the Crescent sits with its quiet public gardens. Up in the older town there remain one or two ancient fishermen's cottages in Queen Street but the shopping area is low key, with a surprisingly large number of Chinese restaurants, café's, independents and charity shops adding to the tranquil and unruffled mood of the place. Sleep on Filey and stay select.

CHAPTER NINE

Lymington and Southsea: salt, sailors, seawater baths and a suburb by the sea

Is Lymington the snootiest town in Britain?
The Guardian, September 2010

It's a mystery why the *Which?* readership decided to include Lymington in its list of seaside resorts, but they did. You would think that a seaside resort needs a beach after all. The score for Lymington's beach isn't even a zero, just a 'not applicable'. Bit strange for a seaside resort but it's true. The Hampshire town may be on a beautiful coastal river inlet but a stroll to the sea involves a windy, exposed walk along a huge embankment looking inland to salt marsh and ponds and out to the Isle of Wight and the busy Solent, full of all sorts of boats and yachts. But no beach.

Lymington's charms are of a different kind to traditional seaside resorts. *Which?* readers loved its scenery, food and drink, shopping options and peace and quiet. You can see and hear why. Not an amusement arcade in sight or sound.

Instead, it is a town of Georgian splendour, slightly smug and self-satisfied with that touch of exclusivity that comes from the presence of a number of marinas, yacht and boating clubs. Popular too, as evidenced by the *Sunday Times* declaring it as one of the country's best places to live in 2018.

It still carry's the imprint of an ancient old layout of large houses along the High Street with long thin plots extending to the rear, known as 'burgages', rented by local citizens for trade and building their homes. Salt and smuggling funded many grand Georgian houses with large sash windows, top floors for servants and bay windows on the first and second floors. Wealth was on display in the buildings of the time. A good example is at Bellevue House, built of bricks in 1798, laid with the ends pointing out, accentuating both the cost, through the number of bricks needed, and also the thickness of its walls.

The snootiest town in Britain

Driving in from Beaulieu you cross the Lymington River (past the rather unique *Otters crossing* sign) and are immediately faced with one of the town's more controversial developments, the curious curving walls of the three storey apartment blocks known as Lymington Shores. These curving walls are a modern pastiche of one of Lymington's more famous features, of which more later. Sitting on the site of an old chicken factory, this development has taken over sixteen years to come to fruition and there are still several outstanding and problematic issues to be resolved to the local resident's satisfaction by developers Redrow.

As one or two other big companies have found, mess with the people of Lymington and you stir up a lot of trouble. Past run-ins with Argos and Wetherspoons, neither regarded by some as the right sort of establishment for the town, have led to public accusations of NIMBYism on a grand scale.

'The snootiest town in Britain' vouched *The Guardian*. 'The town that is too posh for Argos' cried *The Independent*, just as local residents also attempted to see off Wetherspoons in 2011. The pub chain's move, to a building by the parish church in the town centre, attracted over 900 objections. It didn't work. Wetherspoons now have their pub in the town and the reported snobbery of locals hasn't stopped the usual outbreak of charity shops, coffee chains, convenience stores and even a Poundland, lowering the tone amongst Lymington's more pricy offerings. Indeed, the town's mix of shops is a riot of oddities with expensive jewellery, ice cream, spa treatment and sailing outfitters alongside designer pasties, a lot of barbers, lifestyle boutiques and hatters and tailors.

A history of salt and sails

To be fair however, Lymington is different. With a small population of 16,000, including its suburban villages, it has a pleasant Georgian (and Victorian) centre with a wonderful riverside location, lined with marinas. These add a distinctly elitist whiff to the local environment, as well as the constant slap, smack and whistling of steel rigging in the wind.

The town owes its wealthy Georgian heart to the manufacture of salt, a commodity much in demand from the Middle Ages right up to the nineteenth century. The presence of the local salt marshes, plenty of sunshine and low humidity were perfect conditions for the creation and extraction of salt. The first references to salt in the area go back to the Domesday Book and by 1660, the local website *Lymington.com* reported that the town's salt producers were using as much coal as all of London.

The salt was produced by drawing sea water into cut trenches where it evaporated to leave a salty brine. The brine was then taken into tanks, boiled (hence the large use of coal) and the salt skimmed off again, ready for transporting. At its peak in 1730 over 160 salt pans were in use and salt was being distributed around the world. One successful local trader, Charles St Barbe, a famous name in the town, made enormous profits from the trade despite heavy salt taxes. At one time the tax on salt was so high it had reached fifteen times its actual value. The local museum quotes the town providing salt tax revenue of £57,000, about £4 million today.

By the middle of the nineteenth century the town had a population of over 2,300 and was a thriving market town and port. The 1830s in particular saw a flurry of investment as gas street lighting arrived, the open-air seawater baths were built and the first paddle steamer travelled between Lymington and Yarmouth on the Isle of Wight. But the town's salt production gradually died out as the century progressed, due to the rising fuel costs of the enormous amounts of coal needed to boil the pans and cheaper rock salt becoming the favoured material. In 1865 the last salt producer in the town closed down.

As a port Lymington had flourished throughout this time, with the usual bouts of illegal smuggling (of which up to 90% of the townspeople were active, according to Aimee Durnell) mixed in with export and import of goods and a boat building industry.

The port was successful enough to have attracted the attention of the French who attacked it twice in the fourteenth century and once again in the sixteenth century. By the nineteenth century the ship building activity had switched to yachts, of which the Berthon Boat Company became the most well-known and is still in existence today. The Berthon business sits on the first site of the earliest yacht builder, Thomas Inman, dating back to 1820. He was funded by a local landowner and keen yachtsman, Joseph Weld. With his resources Inman became a famous yacht builder and racer himself, building up enough money to buy the shore strip along the Lymington River.

It wasn't just yachts and boats plying their trade up the Lymington River though. Since around 1485 fishermen were carrying passengers over to the Isle of Wight from the town. It took until 1841 for ancient paddle steamers to begin a regular trade and in 1861 the ferry could meet the train at the jetty. Michael Williams reported that the *Lymington Chronicle* of the day protested about the passengers sharing the decks with hundreds of sheep whilst vehicles were transported in separate barges until 1938. Today the *Wightlink* runs sheep-free, to Yarmouth, up to fourteen times a day transporting a million passengers a year.

Welcome to the Club... possibly

In truth there is no avoiding the yachts and yachties of Lymington. The sight and sounds of so many boats, yachts, sailing vessels, chandlers and sailing shops dominates the town and any wander down towards the river draws you to the view across the marinas and boatyards with their endless masts and flapping lanyards. In the summer, during the regatta season, the town positively hums with nautical types of all qualities.

At the start of the twentieth century, boats called 'Lymington prams' (now known as scows) built by the Berthon company, were being sailed in the river. The Lymington River Sailing Club was set up in 1914 to race the prams, only to be closed as war arrived. It reopened in 1922 and began to build membership, until in 1938 it obtained a royal warrant and became the Royal Lymington Yacht Club.

The royal warrant went to the Club's head. Its own proud historical publication seems to fondly recall the time of aspirant members being 'black-balled' as a black ball was dropped into their membership application to prevent them joining. Anyone associated with 'trade' got short shrift and even one recently divorced applicant of the right type found himself black-balled, as the blazered top brass considered him to be the guilty party.

Things aren't quite so elitist these days. The club welcomes new members and proudly spouts on its website the many and varied activities it offers, including being able to eat in its own Mosimans restaurant. Oh yes... but then you must be nominated by two full members, of two years standing, who can vouch for you being 'active on the water'. Then your application sits on the notice board for 28 days 'to inform other members of your wish to join'. Then there might be an interview. A little bit better than a black ball I suppose.

You could of course become an international yachting superstar and multi-gold medal winning Olympian like Ben Ainslie. He is an honorary life member of the Royal Yacht Club, Lymington's first freeman from a time when he lived in the town and has his own gold post box in the High Street. Gold medals ease the passage through the bureaucracy.

Perhaps it's unsurprising that the two other sailing clubs, Lymington Town and Salterns, have a more open and dare I say, less elitist view of membership. Indeed, Salterns is run by children for children who don't need to be 'active on the water'. The Lymington Town club was set up after a public meeting in 1946 because as Jude James quotes, it was felt 'there was room for a club for people who were shipwrights, builders and shopkeepers who might not wish to join the Royal or who could not anyway'.

Wavy walls and sea-bathing

As a quaint and endearing little town, Lymington has its share of eccentricities. A popular curiosity, that has been mimicked by the new developers of the Lymington Shores site, is the so-called wavy wall, or crinkle-crankle wall. The oldest, according to a local Residents Association leaflet, dated back to the early eighteenth century and still exists on Church Lane. Only one brick thick, its curves provided it with strength without buttresses in similar fashion to the curves in corrugated iron, as well as benefiting from fewer expensive bricks. This type of wall was well known to the Hanoverian troops stationed here at the time and the troop commander built it to ensure prying eyes were kept off his soldier's activities.

Local people were quick to pick up on this innovation, especially as many French prisoners of war were available in Portsmouth and Hurst Castle and they could build the walls for free. Remains of these walls still exist in Lymington and Hampshire but the most famous is perhaps that built by the author Denis Wheatley. In 1945 he purchased Grove Place in the town and resolved to build a wavy wall of over two hundred feet along Church Lane. Like Winston Churchill he was a keen amateur bricklayer, even writing a book called *Saturdays with bricks,* dedicated to Churchill.

Without a sandy beach, you would think that the late eighteenth and nineteenth century pastimes of sea-bathing would pass the town by, but strangely, even Lymington got caught up in meeting the demands for dousing yourself in sea water, as long as a hot bath was available afterwards. Beeston's Baths arrived in the 1770s with a bath house offering hot showers later in the 1830s. Despite the investment in the Baths, as Jude James notes, Lymington never really caught on as a watering-place and they were sold to the busy George Inman in 1855 and then the local Council in 1929.

Today the bath house is the home of the Lymington Town Sailing Club, but the town still has the oldest open seawater bathing pool in the UK. The baths were listed in 2012 and now contain, as a feature when open in the summer, the south coast's biggest floating obstacle course.

The party goes on

The Lymington of the nineteenth century boomed as a 'party town' for the gentry and aristocratic army and navy officers, as well as an increasingly well-off middle class. It still had its rougher parts, with twice as many inns and pubs as there are today and the Quay had its share of brothels and heavy drinkers. Over time, it was gradually being transformed into a more cosmopolitan and middle-class place to live as sailing grew in popularity. Today it's popular with the retirement crowd, families attracted by the great location and the 'Swallows and Amazons' offers out on the water, along with the hardy sailing types.

It's not all swanky Georgian homes and expensive boats though. As it's outside the New Forest National Park the town has had its fair share of uninspiring infill developments that have merged the town into the villages of Pennington and Buckland. These have at least served to bring in a larger number of younger families and change the often-inexorable drift of seaside towns becoming havens for older people.

The local Lymington Society continues to fight the good fight for Lymington's Georgian heart, whilst the sailing clubs maintain the sporty outdoor vibe that gives the town its distinctiveness and character. I spoke to local Lymington Society member Donald Mackenzie who has lived in the town for forty years. He sees a 'very bright future for a town recovering from recession' with a growing mix of shops replacing the loss of recession and Covid hit chain stores. He discussed the pressures on the town too. Its popularity has brought house price increases and over enthusiastic developers wanting more sheltered and older persons housing. He quoted that there were twenty-two such schemes in the town already and 'the last thing we need is another sheltered scheme bringing pressure on our public services'. What the town needed, in his view, was more affordable homes.

As a thriving seaside resort, perhaps a beach too.

Southsea: the suburban seaside resort

Southsea is a rather unique suburban resort. Attached to the southern end of the much larger city of Portsmouth, on the nine-mile-long Portsea Island, it was originally built as an escape from the dirt and squalor of the military city and only later in the nineteenth century were its attractions as a seaside resort first developed. Its growth as a resort was also restricted by its tight geographic position with the sea on three sides, the city of Portsmouth to the north and the fact that huge amounts of land were in the Government's ownership. To a large extent these restrictions meant that Southsea retained a distinctive air with its hotels and seaside attractions pushed out away from the coast by the strategic demands of the Government for open land and military sight lines along the sweep of the southern shore.

Indeed, as the Holbrook guide to Southsea and Portsmouth stated in 1899, this government ownership was something to be welcomed as it meant that the 'enterprise of the speculative builder has not been allowed to interfere with the general comfort and convenience'.

Just at the start of the nineteenth century the area now covered by Southsea was a flat, open and marshy area, the centre of which was occupied by a bog called the Great Morass; hardly the most inviting invitation to discerning tourists. It did have at its southern tip, the Southsea Castle, dating from the 1540s and built under the instruction of Henry VIII to protect the port of Portsmouth. This was to be a well-used military installation for nearly 400 years until it was withdrawn from active service in 1960 and bought by the city council.

Croxton and Owen lead the way

The first housing appeared outside of the fortifications of Portsmouth in the early 1800s, away from the poor drainage of the boggy Common and Great Morass. It was a brave move to venture outside the defences of Portsmouth's walls, but a man called Thomas Croxton, quoted by Dr R.C. Riley as perhaps Southsea's first and most successful land speculator, built out the first streets in what became known as Croxton Town. Essentially these were good quality houses for 'artisans' and shipyard workers aspiring to a better life outside of Portsmouth's slums. They were quickly followed by more imposing terraces and grander villas for the suburban gentry of the time.

After 1830, Southsea expanded to the north-east and south-east of Croxton Town, but in contrasting styles. Towards Portsmouth, terraces of housing were laid out in a grid-iron pattern. To the south-east the layout adopted was driven by a new land speculator and visionary who introduced wide and curving avenues with larger individual plots for villas and much more substantial houses. He was Thomas Ellis Owen and it was his stamp on the town that created the middle-class and upper-class enclave that was to give Southsea a Victorian boost.

As Dr Ridley noted, Owen created a suburb more akin to the garden suburbs that were to emerge over thirty years later, with a distinctive style of secluded villas and terraces tucked away on sinuous, quiet roads that led down to the Common. Not everyone was a fan of Owen's plans, however. Nicholas Pevsner, the architectural commentator, considered Owen's villas to be 'strange and awkward'. The Victorians loved them though and many rented the homes owned by Owen, to gain access to the town's burgeoning resort attractions.

Today the roads and terraces of Grove Road, The Thicket, Queens and Clifton Terraces amongst others, are down to

Owen. Whilst redevelopment has seen many of his villas disappear, a number of the Terraces, including what many regarded as his best work, Portland Terrace, still stand and are the town's finest Victorian buildings. Local author William Curtis considered Owen to have built, in just thirty years, a brand-new village with its own unique character unlike anything else on the island.

The growth and development of the Portsmouth dockyard as an employment driver was also key to Southsea's success in the mid 1800s as the city's middle class sought the town's fresher air and sea access for a better quality of life. Indeed, this desire for a high-quality living environment was in Ridley's view, more the reason for improvements to the state of the Common and the arrival of the publicly funded beach promenade in the 1840s, than a wish to attract seaside tourists.

A welcome to tourists

It took up to the 1860s for the trappings of a seaside resort designed to attract visitors, rather than provide a few local pleasures, to really get a grip on Southsea. Initially there seemed to be a lack of confidence in the town as an alluring resort with lodging houses and hotels slow to arrive along the seafront facing the Common. Once Southsea had overcome this recalcitrance it began its quest to attract the right kind of seaside client. In just thirty years from 1860 to 1890, new hotels, the Esplanade, the branch railway line and the Canoe Lake all appeared across the span of land facing the Southsea Common. The essential attribute of any resort, a pier, (today's Clarence Pier) arrived in 1861 offering trips to the Isle of Wight and was such a success it was enlarged in 1869 and 1871. A second pier, at South Parade, was opened in 1879, built to a length to allow ferries to the Isle of Wight to dock alongside.

By the 1870s the local Corporation was busy extending the attractions available with a new sea wall east of Southsea Castle and a lease on the ownership of Lumps Castle, a deteriorating building dating back to the 18th century and built as further protection of the important Portsmouth harbour. Despite this, as Ridley notes, by the late 1800s Southsea continued to retain a 'mature and select' nature with published guides at the time remarking on the 'salubrious air', the 'brightness and lightness of its open spaces', whilst 'a stroll is an object lesson in this country's history'.

We have found that for many resorts it was the arrival of the railway that changed the nature of tourism, bringing in the working-classes and a much wider social group. This wasn't to be the case in Southsea, however. It took until 1885 for an extension linking the railway in Portsmouth to be pushed through to the coast with a terminus close to the South Parade pier. The railway struggled for viability in competition with trams and other transport offers and by 1914 it had closed for good.

Right up to the time of World War One the whole area was dominated by a huge naval and military presence overshadowing any pretence for Southsea to be a 'typical' seaside resort. Sarah Quail stated that by 1914 over twenty-five per cent of Portsmouth's male working population was in uniform. Local people were accustomed to seeing marching men exercising on the Common and the military brought not just a need for outfitters and service essentials but also a huge need for pubs.

In 1923 the Government sold the ownership of the Common to the Council for £45,000 but placed restrictions on development west of Southsea Castle to keep the Common open and undeveloped. A clause retained the ability of the Army to put up billets, muster troops, march and of course, play cricket. The clause was rescinded in 1966 allowing a different set of more amenable uses to appear.

Undoubtedly this helped to maintain Southsea's individuality alongside the retention of the Victorian suburbs and the local corporation's attempts to develop resort attractions to entice visitors into the town. It was also the case that Southsea continued to operate its tourist offer almost independently of Portsmouth despite an administrative link in 1904. As Bateman and Riley pointed out, the promotion of Southsea as a resort was part of a deliberate attempt to separate the tourism and defence functions. The naval connections of Portsmouth were perceived to lack any sort of tourist appeal.

Changing tack on the drive for the tourist pound

Portsmouth and Southsea were both heavily bombed by the Germans during World War Two. In 67 air raids over 900 people were killed. The destruction of the Clarence Pier and residential areas, after the sealing off of the promenades and beach, left Southsea in a precarious position. Coupled with post-war changes in the patterns of holiday-making and defence spending cuts badly affecting the naval presence in the city, the resort faced a progressive decline.

It was also hampered by a limited selection of hotels, indoor attractions and a poor-quality beach. A reputation as a resort for the monied middle-classes worked against it, as this group began to go elsewhere for their holidays. As a result, a shift in the promotion of Southsea as a resort took place in the 1980s, as the town joined with Portsmouth in a new venture: promoting the dockyard and historical heritage alongside Southsea's resort pleasures.

Taking over Southsea Castle was a prompt for this joint action. The town's failure to independently develop a series of grandiose schemes around the Castle made it turn to the idea, with Portsmouth, of a new museum, military and maritime history-led tourism strategy. With the town of Southsea administratively tied to Portsmouth, it made sense to think of the two as one to attract visitors, especially as Southsea's popularity as a 'select' resort waned whilst Portsmouth's maritime tourism grew in importance. It was no longer good enough for Southsea to rest on the laurels of its ageing Victorian attractions to bring in the tourists.

Today's *Which?* guide readers agreed. The beach couldn't be considered as a big draw with just two stars (it's shingle all the way), but the new local attractions got five stars. Investment in indoor draws such as the refurbished D-Day Museum, Exploria soft play centre and Sea Life Centre, (now known as the Blue Reef Aquarium) and new, larger, but cheaper chain hotels, along with the proximity of the new dockyard attractions, such as the Mary Rose and HMS Victory, drew nearly 10 million visitors to the city in 2015. As Nigel Yates pointed out, there was an irony in the arrival of these big seafront attractions some twenty years after the decision to no longer market Southsea alone, as a separate seaside resort.

By 2010 the councillors of the city of Portsmouth, including

Southsea, were declaring that the aim was to be 'a European city break destination with world-class attractions'. The Dockyard, the historic ships and museums and the seafront attractions of Southsea were now marketed as one.

Protecting the future

As tourism took a positive turn, albeit away from the strolling promenading of the Victorians, Southsea had to face up to another threat; the flooding of the low-lying Portsea Island. Climate change and inadequate flood defences mean that up to 10,000 homes, 74 listed monuments, 700 commercial properties and 4.5km of shoreline are threatened by inundation. In 2015 an assessment of the existing sea defences found that they were not expected to last more than ten years in their current condition. Bigger and more significant storms were expected in the future as sea levels rise and waves were regularly washing over existing defences.

The Environment Agency and City Council have combined to invest funds of £100 million into a huge sloping sea wall along the south facing promenade to, in their words, 'hold the line' and aim to use its construction to inspire new investment into hotels, cafes and restaurants. Whilst a lot of land on the Common is being used to house the construction work the hoardings around the site have a rather scary map showing the potential parts of the resort affected by flooding. It's most of Southsea.

Piers, Hovercraft, Monuments and Castles

The resort needs this investment. Today it's certainly not the 'salubrious' town the promenading Victorians enjoyed but it is smartening up. Its Albert Road shopping area is striving to be cool with independents and trendy food options. This contrasts with the recent closures of Debenhams, a smaller John Lewis and other chain stores, which on my visits still sat empty and forlorn in the heart of the retail area.

The Victorian Clarence Pier, opened in 1861, was bombed in 1941 and rebuilt as an unusual pier, far wider than its length, in 1961. The pier now contains a huge gaudy entertainment complex of arcades, slot machines, rides, crazy golf and fast food. Opposite the pier across the Common still stands the Queens Hotel, one of the first in the town and freshly refurbished in the search to become Southsea's first four-star hotel.

To the east of the Pier is the hovercraft access to the Isle of Wight. This offers the world's longest-running commercial hovercraft service and the only scheduled passenger hovercraft service in Europe. Since it was first launched in 1965 it has carried over 26 million passengers the ten minutes to the Isle of Wight. It still a big draw today, with its noisy arrival and departure attracting many watching tourists.

The green sward of the Common opens up and the long (very long) southern promenade stretches down to the Aquarium, D-Day Museum, Southsea Castle, Exploria pyramid and Rock gardens, key attractions for the town, all sitting on the seafront. A host of marine and war memorials line the promenade including the huge Naval memorial commemorating the 24,500 Naval personnel who died in the two World Wars.

As you reach the South Parade, the smartened up Victorian terraces, sympathetic new developments and the refurbished Royal Beach hotel, dating back to 1866, face the vibrant 'family entertainment centre' of South Parade Pier. Opened in 1879 the pier has been burnt down no less than three times, once in 1974 during the filming of the rock musical *Tommy*. After being rebuilt in 1975 it was forced to close amid safety fears in 2012 but then reopened in new splendour in 2017.

Beyond the pier the seafront becomes the Eastney Promenade, passing the Canoe Lake, a seawater lake and the last vestige of the Great Morass which was drained in 1886. By the Canoe Lake is my favourite short road; it's called the 'The Ocean At the End Of The Lane'. Further tourist attractions follow with the Lumps Fort rose gardens, Cumberland House Museum and the Southsea model village. Something for everyone it seems. You can see why the *Which?* readers gave the town's attractions five stars.

For the view of a local resident I spoke to Kevin Dean, Editor and Director of *Southsea Lifestyle,* an online and print magazine. Kevin pointed to the lively and compact nature of the town with a rapidly improving cultural and retail scene, easy access to the Isle of Wight and ever-changing views of the water-borne traffic on the Solent. But he also saw a 'segmented city' where each area saw itself as distinctive and different and lots of people 'wouldn't go to Portsmouth', preferring to use Southsea's facilities or visiting the new 'segment', Gunwharf, for its shops and entertainment, even if 'it was difficult to discern where Portsmouth ends and Southsea starts'. He also regarded the town as a 'poor man's Brighton', cheaper and more working class, with a difficult road system (just two roads lead in and out of Portsea Island) and an insularity that stems from its island location. But he also saw a positive future with millions being spent on the seafront protection and promises of new eco-housing as the town climbed out of its pandemic blues.

Kevin recognised that the future of Southsea as a resort is now intertwined with the success of Portsmouth's maritime tourism irrespective of local residents wish to remain distinctive and different to Portsmouth. The need for continued investment in its seafront and diverse attractions is a key part of the drive to be a 'European city-break destination'.

Whilst the promenading middle-class Victorians used the resort to avoid the muck and squalor of the docks and slums, the future now is less as a unique and select tourist resort than a seaside suburb, with a set of attractions designed to complement those of Portsmouth, drawing tourists to the whole city. Southsea's challenge is to 'stay classy', set apart from Portsmouth for its own culture, history, attractions and seaside ambience whilst benefitting from the investment and draw of the bigger city.

CHAPTER TEN

Bamburgh and Spittal: an astonishing castle and the last beach in England

*It does hit you sometimes, when you least expect,
you look out and you think, wow, aren't we so lucky*

A local Bamburgh resident talks to her
local newspaper about her village

B oy, it's a long way to Bamburgh, on the north-east coast of England, a good 330 miles north of London. It's even further to Spittal, Berwick-on-Tweed's ageing holiday resort, just a few miles south of the Scottish border. These are two distant and isolated seaside resorts. But both are well-loved by our guides, the readers of *Which?*

Bamburgh in particular was awarded five stars for its beach, seafront, attractions, scenery, peace and quiet and value for money. It secured a top five position in 2020 and in 2021 *Which?* readers put it in top place as the best seaside resort in Britain. This was no fluke as it kept its top spot in the 2022 guide. So well worthy of a trip to the beautiful county of Northumberland.

As ever, you must wonder what sort of gin the good readers of *Which?* are drinking though. Five stars for the seafront? Hmm. The beach is stunning and the village's position, beneath the magnificently dramatic Bamburgh Castle, high on a beachside volcanic plug, is truly worthy of its stars, but to be honest, there really isn't a seafront that the traditional resort visitor would recognise. The beach runs on for miles behind the Castle, with no sign of any traditional seafront delights. Inland there is just the Links Road to the south and a narrow road north to the Golf course. All for the better for Bamburgh though. It remains wonderfully unspoilt, isolated and well-preserved.

Bamburgh is not your traditional seaside resort. It is a small and ancient Northumbrian village that just happens to share one of the most dramatically sited castles in Britain, along with a beautiful sandy beach of such a size that even on a busy day it retains a peaceful remoteness the south coast would die for. It won't take long to wander through it either. It only has a population of 450 spread around a handful of narrow streets. You have to ask the question; how come such a small place has dominated the long list of Britain's favourite seaside resorts attracting 150,000 visitors every year?

An ancient home, an impregnable castle and the first welfare state

Bamburgh has long been regarded as a great place to live despite its remoteness. Settlements in the area date back to Neolithic times. A wooden castle was established on the rocky outcrop of the Great Whin Sill by King Ida in 547 AD. Frank Graham, capturing the comments of early written chronicles, describes the scene. 'Bebba (the original name of Bamburgh was Bebba's-burgh after a Queen called Bebba) is a most strongly fortified city not very large, being of the size of two or three fields, having one entrance hollowed out of the rock and raised in steps after a marvellous fashion'. The present castle dates from the twelfth century but still contains the remains of an Anglo-Saxon well, cut through the hard rock of the Whin Sill to a depth of 44 metres, an astonishing and laborious feat at the time and again described in the Chronicle quoted by Graham as having water 'sweet to the taste and most pure to the sight'.

The early village can also lay a claim to be the original site of Christianity in the country after the monk Aidan established a church here in 635 AD and spread the Christian word out from Northumberland. At this time, Oswald, the King who appointed Aidan to establish Christianity in the area, was a hugely powerful figure and it appears that his base in Bamburgh became a cosmopolitan and wealthy settlement. We know this from recent archaeological digs in the dunes by the Castle where many high-status burials took place. Analysis has shown that the buried came from a variety of places including North Africa and the Mediterranean. The *Bamburgh Research Project* discovered the remains in an area known as the Bowl Hole, beneath the Castle. The bones have now been re-interred in the current St Aidans Church crypt in the village.

The stone castle was a defensive bastion against the Scots for 350 years. It became the first castle ever attacked by cannonballs in the War of the Roses but went into a steady decline thereafter as it lost its purpose as a defence against the Scots.

A settlement beneath the castle hosted a large Friary that acquired a large landholding in the area, all of which was seized by Henry VIII in 1545 following the dissolution of the monasteries. For just £664 the castle and land were sold by James I to the Forster family who continued to own it until 1704 when it was acquired by Lord Nathaniel Crewe, the Bishop of Durham.

Lord Crewe and the charitable trust he set up for the village on his death, were to provide a deep and transforming benefit to Bamburgh. The Lord Crewe Trust was to rebuild much of the village that had suffered under the Forsters. Trusteeship of the Trust came to a Dr John Sharp, a member of a fascinating family of talented and innovative siblings.

Under Sharp the Trust established what has been called the first 'welfare state', with a school, hospital, dispensary, a lending library and a welfare centre for shipwrecked mariners. Frank Graham quotes Sharp on why he did this. 'Once a vessel was wrecked behind the castle and the crew saved; but the unfortunate master, having escaped the perils of the sea, died of a damp bed in the village. That, the like may never happen again, all shipwrecked sailors who come are received here and supplied with every necessary. This was the beginning of our little infirmary, which soon suggested the idea of a general dispensary for the poor'.

Dr Sharp was a clever and innovative visionary. It is said that he established the first coastguard system in the country, with a gun fired in bad weather from the castle ramparts and a waking watch on the beach looking out for ships in trouble. It is also claimed that Sharp commissioned the first ever lifeboat in 1786, by requesting an un-sinkable boat from a designer called Lionel Lukin. He cared for the village too and after finding St Aidans church in serious neglect he took on the task, with his descendants, of restoring the building. The Sharp family has a memorial in the church to commemorate their involvement.

By the late 1800s the Trust was failing financially and sold its estate for £60,000 to the Armstrong family, rich industrialists of the time, who have retained their ownership of the Castle and parts of the village to this day. The original purchaser, William Armstrong, was the perfect man to follow in Dr Sharp's footsteps as he too was a pioneering innovator, this time in engineering, water and solar power. He was to spend over £1 million to restore the Castle, a huge sum at the time, originally with the idea of it becoming a convalescent home. His family have taken on his legacy since his death in 1900 and they have restored the Castle completely, turning it into a major tourist and event attraction, hosting many major films including most recently and when I last visited, the latest *Indiana Jones* film.

Armstrong invested in the village too, building Armstrong House, as a rest home for his industrial workers in 1925 and the golf course and its clubhouse to the north of the village in 1904. Armstrong House is today a sheltered housing scheme run by Abbeyfield and the golf course is considered to be one of the most scenic in Britain. Lord Armstrong also had the Armstrong Cottages built on the Links Road, south of the village. These were nineteen single storey homes built for the workmen who refurbished the castle at the turn of the nine-teenth century. They still survive today, refurbished themselves as holiday homes.

It was perhaps the Armstrong's who first saw the potential of Bamburgh as a seaside resort. On opening the new golf links in 1904 and quoted on the golf club website, the then Lord Armstrong stated that 'the only thing wanted to make Bamburgh an ideal holiday resort was a golf links'.

A Victorian heroine

For such a small village Bamburgh's attractions extend well beyond the beautiful beach and its impregnable Castle. The council officers writing the *Conservation area appraisal for Bamburgh* noted its 'aura of departed greatness'. A bit romantic perhaps but they have captured the essence of the place. Although small, it carries a dramatic history from being the seat of Northumbrian Kings and the home of Christianity in England right through to more modern-day heroism with Grace Darling and the modern philanthropy of the investment of the Armstrong family.

The Grace Darling connection comes from the fact that the village was her original home and a selfless local act of heroism was to make her one of Victorian Britain's great heroines. Grace was a lighthouse-keepers daughter. At the age of 23 in 1838, whilst living at the Longstone lighthouse off the Farne Islands she spotted a ship in distress. With her father she rowed out to the shipwrecked boat and managed to save nine of the boat passengers. Her bravery sparked a series of nationally reported stories and she became a Victorian superstar with plays, shows and songs celebrating her exploits. These often eclipsed the fact that she carried out the rescue with her father. In one period of a few days, she had to sit for no less than seven different portrait artists.

The Darlings became one of the earliest victims of 'fake news' and inaccurate reporting as the story became overblown, melodramatic and exaggerated in the hands of some scribes. None of the family greatly enjoyed many of the tales and they did nothing but generate ill-feeling locally.

She was awarded a medal by the organisation that became the RNLI as well as garnering financial donations from a grateful public and even a sum from Queen Victoria. Grace died of tuberculosis just four years later and is buried in the churchyard of St Aidans with a memorial tomb placed at the churchyards highest point so passing ships can spot her. Bamburgh has a lovely museum dedicated to her too. Initially built in 1938 it is now a modern environmentally friendly attraction and even has the original coble Grace rowed out to the shipwreck.

The church of St Aidan is a popular visit too. It has a history that matches that of the village of Bamburgh and a thirteenth century crypt with a set of spooky Anglo-Saxon bones. The crypt was only discovered by accident in 1837, according to Graham's history of the village, when repairs were being made to the church.

Quintessential England by the sea

The village itself tends to doze peacefully away. When the day-trippers leave you get the feeling that, once again, the popularity of the place has led to a takeover by second-home-owners and it was unsurprising to find out that today around 35% of the village's houses are second and holiday homes. Local people have complained that, during the day, the sheer popularity of the place has led to it being over-run with traffic, careless parking and ambling tourists. The *Daily Mail* reported one resident in May 2022 saying that you could hear 'the collective moan as it was named best seaside resort in the UK'.

It's not difficult to see how an influx of tourists can badly affect such a small place. Bamburgh's wonderful cricket green, dating back to 1860 and sat right below the commanding rock face and walls of the castle, could actually be in the heart of a quintessential rural village. This is indeed part of the village's mystery. You can't see the beach or the sea from within the village and it comes to you as a surprise as you round the Whin Sill rock of the castle and walk through the dunes.

Apart from the dramatic pleasures of the beach, the castle and the Darling Museum, the village offers a peaceful drink in its pubs and cafés, and a terrific sausage sandwich or meat pie from the ever-popular Carter's butcher shop. It's most un-seasidey but all the better for it. A bit of rural Englishness tucked away by the beach.

The last beach in England

Spittal likes to market itself as having England's most north-ernmost beach. Berwick-upon-Tweed might like to challenge that as it lies just a few miles further north and has a couple of small sandy bays accessible from the town and its huge static caravan sites, but they don't compare with Spittal's magnificent sweep of sand so let's give this rather strange little resort the benefit of the doubt.

I say strange, because Spittal is an odd one, almost ambivalent about its natural seaside charms with much of the town turning its back to the sea and possessing a history dominated by fishing and industry as much as tourism. I doubt it's on many tourist lists as a must-visit resort these days either. Despite a wonderful promenade running the length of the beach, its attractions are limited to a new splash park and an ageing 'fun park' and pavilion. It's not going to keep the kids happy for long and once the strollers have walked the promenade the fantastic history, walls and ancient town of Berwick-on-Tweed beckon you over.

It must be the attractions of Berwick that caught the eye of the *Which?* readers rather than those of the resort of Spittal to be honest. The beach and shopping got pretty short shrift, but the readers loved the scenery, peace and quiet and value for money. Spittal doesn't have much to offer when it comes to these last three criteria so it must have been Berwick that convinced the readers of *Which?* Spittal has a history of fishing and pretty obnoxious industry, both of which have departed to leave an overgrown village more akin to a decaying industrial suburb than a tourist haven.

Spittal lies just a mile from the larger town of Berwick-on-Tweed, sitting to the south of the mouth of the river Tweed with its huge beach stretching south from Spittal Point. It was always a markedly different place to the walled and historically significant border town of Berwick and that difference continues today. Berwick is polishing its historical connections, smartening up its ancient buildings and walls and promoting itself as a visitor attraction. Spittal is very much second best and to be honest, if you didn't already know about its beach and promenade, you probably wouldn't venture south from Berwick. In contrast to Berwick, it's also never been a part of Scotland, as the constant to and fro of the border between the two countries over a period of around 500 years, left the settlements south of the Tweed firmly in England.

The long goodbye to the herring

The name Spittal comes from an Old English shortening of the name for a long vanished medieval hospital. The hospital link continues through the presence of North and South Greenwich roads in the town. The land here was once owned by Greenwich Hospital in London. The Hospital had acquired estates from the Earl of Derwentwater back in the eighteenth century.

From the thirteenth century Spittal was a fishing village, focused on herring and salmon with some mining of coal pits on the nearby Tweedmouth Moor. By the nineteenth century the herring curing business was dominated by Robert Boston (later Boston Brothers) sited on the Sandstell Road at Spittal's northern end. At its peak Menuge and Dewar reported that Bostons employed over 100 people in several curing sheds. Fishing was of paramount importance to the towns of Berwick, Tweedmouth and Spittal during the eighteenth and nineteenth centuries. Salmon and herring could be dried, salted, smoked, pickled or packed in ice and was hugely popular up and down the country. The *friendsofberwick* website reports that huge government bounties on big catches brought a boom time to Spittal right through to the early 1900s.

Spittal still possesses an old fishing shelter, known as a 'shiel' for salmon fishermen and their nets, at the north end of the town. It dates back to 1735 and is now managed by the local charity, the Spittal Improvement Trust. Fishing rapidly declined by the 1930s with a consequent huge drop in herring curing, due mainly to over-fishing.

Mixing fishing and industry with a judicious drop of tourism

Spittal's curious entry into tourism was kicked off once again by the affluent local gentry's pursuit of clean and supposedly healthy spa water. Indeed, the desire for clean water and fresh air was to outstrip the ability of the village of fishermen to provide a decent place to stay. The Spa Well, still sited in the centre of the town, became so popular that as Menuge and Dewar reported, by 1799, 'many who have come to drink it have been obliged to go home for want of lodgings'.

In the early nineteenth century a few large houses were built by the seafront to accommodate visitors. By 1829, an engraving of the time, quoted by Menuge and Dewar, showed promenading visitors mixing with salmon and herring fishermen and horse-drawn coal wagons along the foreshore. Spittal's curious resort status was underway, led by a very local group of well-to-do Victorians from the Scottish Borders and Northumberland. Visiting was also given a boost by the arrival of a cheap ferry to Berwick, followed by the railway extensions from Newcastle to Tweedmouth in 1847 and a branch line from Kelso in 1851. Despite this hardy group visiting Spittal, as Michael Cullen reports, it never did attract sufficient confidence and investment to break into the resort big league.

In 1835, Spittal and its neighbour Tweedmouth were absorbed into the administration of Berwick. It was about this time that the town moved to another stage in its development as heavy industry arrived at Spittal Point. Previously an open area of land edged by the Tweed and the seashore, Menuge and Dewar identified that the Point first housed a gaslight company and then within fifty years, four chemical manure plants and a separate one producing vitriol, or sulphuric acid. *Secret Spittal* reported that in the 1940s these plants were amalgamated under Fisons ownership. Main Street in the town also held a couple of foundries, now demolished. Hardly nice neighbours for a seaside resort, but the prevailing winds did carry the smell out to sea, most of the time. Relief came in the 1950s when the plants closed down as ever-larger ships couldn't negotiate the tricky Tweed Dock and shifted to the bigger port at Immingham.

The towns development to the south of the industrial Spittal Point, down the Main Street and away from the manure plants, was initially known as New Spittal as small villas and terraces appeared, often facing away from the sea. This rather odd layout was probably due to the presence of the Berwick Pier railroad tracks which ran along the seaward side of Main Street right up to 1860. But it was also a different world to the industrial yards and fisherman's cottages cramped around Spittal Point. Michael Cullen points to the growth of over thirty lodging-houses in the town by the mid 1860s, as development spread south.

It is still the case today that much of Spittal's housing appears focused on the Main Street, turned away from the seashore. Only the long St Helens Terrace, built in 1897 by the Boston family (the herring curer), faces the sandy beach and open sea. All this odd development serves to give Spittal the appearance of town that doesn't really want to be a seaside resort, shunning its superb beach views and only bothering to use its seashore for promenaders who want to take a stroll or access the beach itself.

The promenade along the beach was built in two parts, according to *Secret Spittal,* from 1894 to 1899, but it took until

1922 for the only significant beachside construction to take place with the Victorian Pavilion completed by the ice-cream producing Forte brothers. It's still there today, providing an arcade and fast food to passing promenaders. In the 1930s the promenade also offered a putting green, tennis courts and bowls

Spittal wasn't without its occasional celebrity visitors though. The charms of the beach and the town of Berwick were well known to L.S. Lowry, the artist, who visited Berwick from the 1930s right through to just before his death in 1976. There is an excellent Lowry trail to follow that includes examples of the more than thirty pictures, sketches and drawings he drew in Berwick and Spittal. These include *Spittal Sands* in 1960, *Man looking out to Sea* in 1964 and *Girl in a red hat,* on the promenade in 1966. The Berwick Museum and Art Gallery will host its first permanent Lowry too; *Beach Scene,* a picture of Spittal beach and dunes from 1960.

A different future

Spittal today has lost all its heavy and smelly industry, with a sole and lonely chimney left standing sentinel over the cleared ground of Spittal Point. The fishing shiel on Sandstell Road is the last reminder of a once great herring and salmon business and the old fish-gutting sheds have been given over to the Berwick Sailing Club. But at least Forte Brothers, the ice-cream makers, still operate in the town. The promenade has been refurbished and the Forte Brothers Victorian Pavilion is still going, alongside a new addition to the town, a splash park for young children. Many plans have been mooted for the open Spittal Point site, but this distant northern corner has taken its time to attract the investment needed to regenerate such a wind-swept spot. The current plans are for a local businessman to bring in housing and commercial space, but Spittal continues to hold its breath.

The Main Street is a wide road with a lot of character and substantial Victorian buildings and smaller cottages, enhanced by some tall trees, long front gardens and locally added planting. This street and its linking network of roads do provide Spittal with a distinctive feel, disconnected to its neighbours, Tweedmouth and Berwick. Having said that, as a resort it remains a curiosity, a forgotten piece of Victoriana, now left to the local people with an eye for a good beach and stroll. It seems to have lost its purpose really. The fishing has gone, the industry has gone and most of the tourists too. England's northernmost beach is now just one for the curious wanderer with a future dependent on the strength of its local community rather than its appeal to a resort-sated public.

I talked through this perception with Mike Greener, a Town Councillor and Secretary of Spittal Improvement Trust, the local voluntary community group. Despite having lived in the town for thirty-five years Mike still regards himself as an incomer and took the view, as it was throughout Berwick, that it was often the incomers who wanted to see the community thrive and develop. He didn't disagree that Spittal's resort days had waned but made the point that many Scots from the Borders area still visit regularly and the many caravan parks around the Berwick and Spittal area still bring in the day-trippers.

Mike felt the town had in many respects been 'held back', suffering from being in Berwick's tourist shadow and gradually

161

starved of development and services. The genesis of the local community group came from this feeling and the signs of investment in the Point sites reflected his more positive perception of the future for Spittal. I wish him luck. After generations of fishing, heavy and smelly industry and a brief period as a resort for the well to do of the Scottish Borders, Spittal's future may well be to relax into a becoming a secret day-tripper's refuge for a blowy northern stroll.

CHAPTER ELEVEN

Folkestone and Hastings: entrepreneurship on the south coast

We need to set our sights high - it needs vision and it needs courage

Roger de Haan, Folkestone's favourite philanthropist, discusses his plans for the town

. A paradise in concrete and chrome

A commentator's views on the work of Sidney Little, the 'Concrete King' who redeveloped the Hastings seafront

I quite like a flat white coffee. So, it appears, do the residents and visitors of Folkestone and Hastings, two south coast resorts that have fallen on hard times and then been dragged up into a cultural renaissance that has created an effective third life following their Edwardian and Victorian heydays, late twentieth century collapse and current revival.

Coffee seems to be a driver, but then to be honest, many resorts are filling up with thriving independent and chain coffee shops. But something else is happening and much of it driven by entrepreneurs and risk-takers, investing in towns that needed a lift but still carried that seaside *je-ne-sais-quoi,* combined with cheaper accommodation, London accessibility, a rejuvenated local spirit, quirky retail and a heavy dose of cultural regeneration.

Which? readers in 2020 seemed a bit unimpressed with it all however, dumping both resorts into the bottom quarter of the resort table. Although they liked Folkestone's seafront and food options, they didn't go for the value for money it offered or the local shopping. Hastings came off worse with readers disliking the beach (it's stoney), the seafront, value for money and the lack of peace and quiet. Neither resort improved the readers score in 2021. A fickle bunch I would say. There is much to enjoy in both towns.

Folkestone: revival and regeneration

Folkestone is a resort that's been very up, very down and is now certainly back up again. It's an unusual town, dumped into poverty and depression by a combination of changing holiday habits and the closure of its port, but then propelled, almost single-handedly into a cultural and development renaissance by one man, Roger De Haan, a local entrepreneur with vision and a lot of money.

Today Folkestone is a media darling, attracting all the hippest commentators, writers and artists who wax lyrical about its Triennial Arts Festival, the permanent art exhibited around the town, its colourful restored buildings, performing arts venues, destination restaurants, revitalised seafront promenade and exciting new harbour side developments, not to mention the independent coffee shops. In a bid to become the hippest place in the south it now has F51, the world's first multi-storey skate park, the expansion of the Creative Quarter offering low-rent commercial and creative opportunities, a second stage of residential harbour front homes in 'scalloped curves reminiscent of Regency terraces' (as described by the developers) and the renovation of the Leas funicular water lift, branded as the 'worlds slowest white-knuckle ride'. So, there is a lot going on.

Folkestone certainly has the appearance of being a thriving and vibrant place, if not completely abiding to the traditional regeneration spirit of other rejuvenated resorts. It doesn't possess the beaches or architecture of other seaside towns; the shopping streets are in the words of magazine *Harpers Bazaar* 'steadfastly and resolutely plain' and it still has some down at heel hotels and decaying buildings. But the old Edwardian charms still exist in the Leas, the gardens, bandstands and of course, the Grand Hotel, all boosted by the busy work of the *Creative Folkestone* initiative and the philanthropy and entrepreneurship of the de Haan family.

An Earl and a King

Folkestone burst onto the seaside resort scene in just one short decade in the 1840s. A tourist guide of 1848 ventured the opinion that just eight years earlier the town 'was approaching its decay and whose name would shortly be mentioned as a place that had been, but whose site alone was remembered'. A combination of fortuitous factors transformed the town. As the 1848 guide put it 'the wand of the railway wizard was waved over it and Folkestone was resuscitated'. Money and development swiftly followed, driven by the investment of a local landowner, the Earl of Radnor.

Well before the arrival of the de Haan family, Folkestone was to benefit from this wealthy Earl with a vision to radically change the place from its early nineteenth century fishing village origins. The Earl of Radnor owned a large estate in Folkestone and with the arrival of the railway in 1843, he took the opportunity to develop his land with architect designed stucco terraces and villas, to deliberately attract a high-quality visitor. The Earl's family, the Bouveries, were originally of Huguenot descent from the Netherlands and based in Wiltshire but exploited the Folkestone estate carefully and deliberately.

In 1844 a branch of the railway was extended to the harbour and eventually this allowed rail passengers to alight and immediately join the sailings to France, further boosting trade to Folkestone and the development of the harbour.

By the 1850s the town had doubled in size and the Earl saw his West Cliff estate developed with wide tree lined streets, public and private squares and gardens. New hotels were built, shops constructed up the Tontine Road and by 1868, warm sea-water baths were built to provide safe bathing. This latter innovation brought the fashionable punters rolling in and Folkestone quickly became the county's, if not the south's grandest resort. The wealthy needed somewhere to promenade and show off, so extensive gardens were laid out along the Leas and Sandgate Road. To maintain that exclusive air, the Earl employed private policemen to keep out the wrong sort of visitor.

Folkestone needed attractions to keep visitors occupied. A camera obscura arrived in 1886, the Victoria pier in 1888, the Leas water powered funicular in 1885 and a switchback elevated railway in the 1890s. This last innovation caused much consternation to the local wealthy residents who felt it was the sort of thing the hoi-polloi would come to the town to use. Even the arrival of a bandstand on the Leas caused a fuss. It took forty years to come to fruition in 1895 after local residents had objected to it blocking their view.

By the end of the nineteenth century Folkestone was the most fashionable and desirable resort on the south coast. The completion of two huge new hotels, the Grand and the Metropole, were to mark the pinnacle of the resort's popularity. According to the local Heritage Strategy the Grand was built by a builder who was so upset not to get the Metropole contract he built his own hotel right next door. It was purportedly the first building in the world to have a steel frame in-filled with reinforced concrete and its quality quickly became a favourite with King Edward VII. It's also alleged that Agatha Christie wrote *Murder on the Orient Express* in the hotel, despite there being no mention of Folkestone in her own biography.

Perhaps the clearest indication of what Folkestone was trying to achieve came with the lease in 1902 for the Leas Pavilion tearoom. It specifically stipulated that the tearoom be for 'the highest-class tea and refreshment trade with the view to securing the best class of visitors only'.

A town in decline

The First World War was to bring a complete change to Folkestone. The fashionable wealthy visitor numbers dried up as the hotels and boarding houses were requisitioned for refugees. The wealthy were not to return, preferring to go abroad as European travel opened up. Folkestone had to go down market, reaching out to a middle-and-working class family orientated audience. To meet this new clientele new amusement facilities and a heated swimming pool were constructed, along with a dance hall and pleasure gardens.

Edwina Keown, writing in *Modernism on Sea* spoke of the turn to commerciality with 'Dainty Afternoon Teas, Bouncing Dillon's Comedy Gymnasts, Strong Men Wrestling and Ladies Orchestras'. Even the very first seaside beauty contest. Oh dear.

The Second World War set Folkestone back again. The town became a restricted access zone and the population fell by over 10,000 to 35,000. Many buildings were bombed and the Victoria Pier was broken up, ultimately destroyed by a fire in 1945 and demolished nine years later.

Whilst the 1950s saw its tourist popularity rise again with the Rotunda amusement arcade reopening and floral displays returning, this decade was to be the last where traditional seaside attractions brought the punters in to the town. As the 1970s rolled in, Folkestone suffered in the same way as many other British resorts. Holidaymakers went elsewhere and the resort declined as revenues dropped, attractions became outdated and unloved and the town became poorer and more dilapidated.

The town attracted some bizarre investment from those with forlorn hopes of changing its direction of travel, most notably the arrival of the Grand Burstin Hotel on the site of the late lamented Royal Pavilion Hotel. The Grand Burstin, resembling a giant concrete cruise liner beached on the shoreline, has attracted its fair share of critics and not just for its architectural style. Online reviews show that the hotel's customers don't seem to like the service on offer.

One iconic but dominant building in the town, Number One, The Leas, built in 1971, did make a successful conversion from an office block to residential flats in the 1980s but its position right on the cliff top in the centre of the town draws the eye into a collection of architectural misfits worthy of wholesale redevelopment.

Another nail in the town's economic coffin came with the completion of the Channel Tunnel in 1994, making the port with connections to France virtually redundant. By the turn of the twentieth century the last cross-channel ferry departed and the port closed.

The town began to display the classic symptoms of many seaside resorts. Kennell found that it had a number of pockets in the town's centre and east, where poverty levels were in the worst 1% of the whole country. He also reported that despite a fall in job availability and an increase in unemployment to twice the national average, the population rose by 6% between 1995 and 2005, mirroring the direction many seaside resorts were taking. Predominantly this growth was driven by poorer households moving into old bed and breakfast hotels that were being broken into flats and an influx of older incomers seeking seaside retirement.

A change for the better

In 2002 the arts charity initiative *Creative Folkestone* was launched and boosted by the decision of local entrepreneur Roger de Haan to invest £60 million in a Creative Quarter of acquired buildings in the town centre. The de Haan family had been important to Folkestone since the end of the War when Sidney de Haan established the Saga company, perhaps most famous for selling holidays to the over-50s. His son, Roger de Haan, sold his business in 2004 for around £1.35 billion. Sidney and Roger had already set up the Roger de Haan Charitable Trust in 1978 and Roger de Haan began using his money through a series of investments and developments in the town.

There is no doubt that that this modern-day philanthropist has made a huge difference to Folkestone. As well as the Creative Quarter, the Trust has invested in education, wildlife, sports, playgrounds and local and county-based organisations. The Trust has been keen to ensure that all aspects of Folkestone society benefit from its support and de Haan himself wanted to ensure that rents in the Creative Quarter remained affordable by controlling the freeholds in the Trust. He also understood the power of education in ensuring a town's future and supported a new City Academy for the town, to retain talented young people in the area with links to the Creative Quarter.

In 2004 de Haan bought the Harbour from the Sea Containers company and began a hugely successful regeneration of the whole station and harbour arm. It is now a 'destination' for the strolling, eating and drinking public. It mixes a very tasteful station refurbishment complete with its original dual language signs with a range of independent food, drink and entertainment venues.

Creative Folkestone has also expanded its repertoire, running Quarterhouse, a performing arts venue, the annual book festival and the Triennial, a massive exhibition of newly commissioned artwork, using the town as a vast open-air gallery. This hugely successful arts initiative, combined with the host of permanent displays, has given the place the largest urban outdoor collection of contemporary art in the country. All sorts of sculpture by artists such as Tracy Emin and Antony Gormley, vibrantly painted beach huts, colourful mock holiday homes and even murals by artist duo Gilbert and George are everywhere, so much so that many have become an unnoticed part of the urban fabric.

After the first Triennial in 2008 it has recently celebrated its fifth, with a burst of yet more temporary installations across the town. These lure in not just an arty crowd. According to the *National Coastal Tourism Academy*, over seventy-five different foreign press teams have poured into the town along with good old fashioned seaside tourists and locals hungry for a little extra with their fish and chips.

Trouble is that art can't save a town on its own. It was a point well made by Alastair Upton, the Chief Executive of Creative Folkestone in 2019, to the *Independent*. Poverty and social inequality need a set of more structural and national interventions. Upton identified 530 different creative businesses in the town from dressmaking to dancers, graphic designers to artists but he was keen to stress the wider impact that the cultural revolution has had on the local population by making the art both accessible and free.

There is still a need to invest in many of the town's other older tourist facilities too. The Leas water powered lift is a case in point. It may be a rare example of its type, but it closed in 2010 and currently needs over £3.5 million to fund its restoration. Even the wonderful Grand Hotel, once the centre of Folkestone's royal tourism business, now needs millions of pounds spent on repair costs. The building today consists of individually owned apartments with several dilapidated communal areas needing considerable investment from the new freeholders, the residents themselves.

As with so many of the resorts we have visited, the future for these projects can lie with a mix of local entrepreneurial spirit chasing grants and scarce funds or a combination of big residential investment supporting the regeneration of older tourist gems. The Leas pavilion is a case in point. A rare example of an Edwardian purpose-built tearoom, after closure in 2010, its restoration is now dependent on the addition of a nine-storey luxury apartment block above it.

A change too far?

De Haan and his money are now at work on the Harbour front with a £350 million plan to build 1,000 homes, shops, restaurants, sports facilities and gardens, masterminded by leading architect Sir Terry Farrell. The first buildings are going up, right on the seafront where the Rotunda fairground once stood by the Leas lift. The rippling white tiled structure will not be to everyone's taste but the views to France are to die for.

Transformative as it is, the plan has come in for criticism as it is likely to bring in wealthier residents and leave the locals out. The *Guardian* reported in 2016 on regeneration expert James Kennell's comments that the new developments were 'not for local people. All the primary benefits are for people moving in or for visitors'. In the same article, Jonathan Ward, a university sociology researcher was more cutting. He said that that arts spending was 'a bit of cultural branding used to conceal what is basically a speculative development aimed at elite customers'.

Perhaps too harsh, given de Haan's commitment to transforming the town as a place to live and his investment in the local community and education. Of course, there will be questions around how this huge new development and the tourism boost it is bringing to Folkestone will actually help local people, but it's difficult in my view, to be churlish over such a transformation. So much of this town has been built around the tourism business since the 1840s and without the de Haan entrepreneurship, it could have continued its decline, with the tourists and jobs deserting.

In some respects, Folkestone is a bit of a schizophrenic town. In part colourful, vibrant, busy and eclectic, driven by new developments and creativity in the arts and then in part down at heel, still struggling with issues of deprivation, poor housing and a substandard retail centre away from the colourful independents in the *Creative Quarter*. The town's Coastal Communities Team has spotted this split identity and has sought to develop a common brand for the whole place. The hope for Folkestone is that its arts, creativity and physical regeneration alongside its distinctive heritage seaside assets can propel the whole town into a much brighter future.

The battle for Hastings

Poor Hastings. Every time a media reporter hits the town, they always seem to slip into their headlines the easy cliché of a battle for this or that in the town. The real Battle of Hastings took place well outside the town but after so many centuries it has always been Hastings that carried the name of England's most dramatic defeat.

Battles there are though, in this historic and eclectic seaside resort. Without the philanthropy of a de Haan anywhere in sight, this is a town that has been launching a series of local battles to both preserve and revive itself as a resort, whilst trying to secure the town as a viable and sustainable community that supports its strangely diverse population. Nothing works easily or simply here in Hastings. Investment comes and goes. Ideas wax and wane. Chaotic and weird, is how some locals have described it themselves.

What sticks is down to a resilient local community, capable of building schemes out of small pockets of cash but buckets of hope and creativity. To understand what's been going on we take a ride through the highs and lows of Hastings and the plans to revive a troubled economy and community.

The end of the Pier?

Let's begin with the Pier. In the 1960s the pier was a popular music venue hosting the Rolling Stones, Jimi Hendrix and many other top rock and pop bands. The 1980s marked a change as the pier's popularity waned and it began a steady decline as new owners, some dodgier than others, bought it and passed it on. Little investment in the structure led to the Council forcing its closure in 2006, to the dismay of Hastings folk. In 2010 around 95% of the pier was destroyed in a fire. Even this didn't dampen the spirits of local people who continued to seek new funds, through a local charity, to completely rebuild the pier as a community asset. By 2016 they had achieved their aim, with over £14 million going into a wonderful new architect-designed pier that broke the traditional mould.

In 2017 the renovated and delightful pier won the Stirling Prize as the best British building project of the year. Rightly so, as it was a masterpiece of understatement, with a huge, uncluttered boardwalk stretching out into the sea. It was to be 'the town square that Hastings doesn't have' according to its architect, Alex de Rijke. Funded by the Heritage Lottery Fund it also attracted individual donations from over 3,000 people.

But then, in the very same year, things started to go wrong. The charity running the pier went into administration, unable to fund its running costs. A local crowd-funding campaign raised insufficient funds to take it on and in 2018, a local businessman, Abid Gulzar bought it for, allegedly, just £60,000.

Sadly, he was not to be the pier's saviour. His reported interest in gold 'bling' in his other hotel and pier investments brought some strange gold lions to the pier, but he closed the pier's doors in December 2018, citing maintenance issues. The people of Hastings were frustrated and flummoxed. All this public and individually donated cash had come to nought. Many commentators reported on the anger and resentment the Gulzar purchase had created, especially as it was seen as a community asset and not one to be privately controlled.

Despite the pier reopening in April 2019, disputes rumbled on as Gulzar brought in kid's amusements and concession shops selling wellness lattes and donuts to generate income, drawing criticism from the scheme's original architects. The sweep of the boardwalk is now covered with picnic tables more at home in a pub garden. Today the pier has a ray of hope, as a music events company has taken a three-year lease to use it for open-air events, turning the clock back sixty years to the music heydays of the 1960s. But Gulzar remains the owner and the people of Hastings maintain a wary watch on his plans for 'their pier'.

'No Jerwood on the Stade'

The pier has always been regarded as a prized local asset. Not so the next big initiative to arrive in the town, the Jerwood Gallery, or as it's known today, the Hastings Contemporary. 'No Jerwood on the Stade' were the signs that greeted plans by the Jerwood Foundation, a private charity, to build an art gallery right by where the much-loved fishing fleet of the town lands its boats. The land was donated by the Council and the rest of the cost was funded by the charity, but the good people of the town didn't all roll over and welcome this largesse.

In part, it was seen as yet another example of how cultural regeneration was aimed at a different and well-to-do group of visitors, offering nothing to the growing poverty of the town. It was also the location that riled the locals, right on the seafront next to the stark black net huts of the Stade with their beached fishing boats, taking up a busy car park site much used by visitors and strangely loved locally. Not a good start for an injection of money and art into Hastings fading grandeur.

'If we are having it, put it somewhere else', was the cry. Up in the town several buildings were becoming dilapidated and worse for wear. Locals saw the gallery as an opportunity to rejuvenate parts of the town that tourists weren't visiting.

It wasn't to be though, and the Jerwood arrived in 2012, gaunt and dark, matching the neighbouring fishing sheds. That's until the massive seagulls launched their white streaked attacks on the shiny blank walls. The gallery needed a lot of financial help and over the next four years the Jerwood Foundation pumped money in. Then, in 2016, the Foundation shocked the town by announcing the withdrawal of its funding support by the end of 2019. A blame game blew up as the gallery hired heavy hitting lawyers to pursue, what it considered to be, contractual obligations to continue funding, as well as a nasty dispute over the use of the Jerwood name. All to no avail.

The Jerwood Foundation pulled its entire collection from the building in 2019 but allowed a new charity to take on the lease of the building, who renamed it the Hastings Contemporary. With new Art Council and philanthropic funding, it now has a focus on local art and the work of the creative sector in the town, but for the people of Hastings, it's yet another example of the money tap turning on and off in the town, as distant investors take decisions that offer no long-term commitment to the town's sustainability.

The disappearing University

Hastings seems to be cursed by such decision-making. Two more examples show how the town has suffered from the power of external interference. Let's start with education. Many seaside towns in decline have benefitted from an injection of university and student spending and Hastings jumped on this bandwagon back in 2005 with the opening of a sponsored University campus in an old telephone exchange.

Brighton University supported the project and great plans for 2,000 students were mooted, with £10 million of regeneration cash going into new buildings, including a grand new centre at Priory Square. Two other buildings on Havelock Road, one funded through SEEDA (the South East England Development Agency) now known as Sea Change (and well known in the town as another disruptive force upsetting the locals), were bought by the University and prospects looked good for the future.

However, Hastings struggled to attract the numbers of students it needed for a viable university campus and in 2015, a new Vice Chancellor of the University announced the intended closure of all its facilities. Despite a huge local campaign to retain the campus, the University held firm and the final students left in the summer of 2019. Not all was lost, as the East Sussex College continues to run University level courses, but there is no doubt that the closure was a body blow to the town's regeneration hopes. Some of its buildings still stand empty awaiting new owners and the hopes for student accommodation investment in a few decaying buildings went out of the window.

The battle for 'our fish'

From one huge topic, education, to another; Brexit. What was meant to be a success story for Hastings fishermen has rapidly turned into another local calamity with cries of betrayal from the town's remaining fishing fleet.

Fishermen have beached their boats at the Stade in the town for over a thousand years and the twenty-five remaining boats still have the right to land free of charge on the stoney beach. Relations with the Council, who claimed ownership of the beach in a much-disputed case with the fishermen that took from 1937 to 1947 to resolve, worsened after the War when a wholesale redevelopment of the fishing area was proposed but eventually rejected.

The fishermen are still on the beach today, the largest shore launched fleet in Europe scattered amongst rusting tractors and decaying abandoned boats. As the boats must be hauled onto the beach, they can't be bigger than ten metres in length. Whilst this means there are many small attractive boats to look at, this does limit catch size and the fishermen have always argued that their fleet operates sustainably as a result.

There was great support from Britain's fishermen to leave the EU in the Brexit referendum, to rid them of what they considered to be the restrictive practices of the Common Fisheries Policy. However, Government assurances turned to dust as promises to control the twelve-mile fishing zone failed to materialise. Paul Joy, a local Hastings fisherman, told *Sussex Bylines* that 'the Government has sold them down the river'.

Huge European trawlers still scour the twelve-mile zone and perhaps in the ultimate irony, of the fish still landed in Hastings, a huge proportion is exported to France. But necessity is the mother of invention. Faced with the post-Brexit problems and the Covid disruption, the fishermen have turned to local shops to try and sell more fish and also utilise the less popular types they catch. They have also expanded their influence with their own fish market, co-operative shop, a charity and a local museum.

Small as it is, the fishing industry in Hastings punches above its weight with huge local support. The brass plaques on the museum commemorating the young men lost at sea are a symbol of that emotional tie. What the fishermen are trying to do is ensure this is not just built around nostalgia but a set of sound, viable, business practices that can insulate it from the failures of post-Brexit decision-making. All very well, but ironically many of the improvements to the unique net sheds on the Stade, the machinery to pull up the boats and the development of the fish market actually came from EU funds pre-Brexit. Perhaps the rejection of the EU is another example of the investment tap in Hastings being turned off.

Hastings fights back

I could go on. Hastings seems to attract publicly or privately funded disasters that need local inspiration to resolve and rebuild. I found numerous examples of local residents' complaints over the use of public money spent by Sea Change, a not-for-profit off-shoot of the old SEEDA, the South East Economic Development Agency. Before it became Sea Change it was known as Sea Space and the organisation had frustrated many local ideas to develop a site in the Ore Valley for community-led housing.

But all is not lost. These frustrations and knock-backs have generated within the town a number of community-based charities, initiatives and festivals that are trying to keep things local, ridding the town of the external conditional investment that blows hot and cold with the seasons.

Heart of Hastings Community Land Trust is a local group working to provide affordable housing and workspaces in the town. It has taken on a well-known building at 12 Claremont as a community asset transfer from the County Council to improve and refurbish and is involved in grant awards for historic buildings in the town centre.

Then there is White Rock Neighbourhood Ventures, a social enterprise developing difficult and derelict buildings into capped rent homes and workspaces. It already has three buildings in its portfolio, either completed or in progress, including the successful Rock House, which provides six low rent flats and six floors of creative working and meeting space.

Inspiration comes in many forms too. Who would have thought that converting a 150-year-old Victorian Turkish baths into the world's largest underground skate and BMX park was a goer? Two brothers, Marc and Rich Moore took on the challenge and raised over £1 million of public funds to convert the building beneath the seafront, renaming it the Source. It now has a shopping gallery too and has revitalised a once abandoned area of the White Rock sea front.

Further along the seafront in St Leonards is another example of local people fighting back. The huge Art Deco mansion block of Marine Court was built to resemble the vast ocean liner, the Queen Mary, and at the time of its completion in 1938, it was the tallest residential building in the UK. By the 1990s the block was needing extensive repairs and the managing agents were declared bankrupt. The residents themselves took to the courts to enforce enfranchisement and take on the block's huge renovation costs. Today it's another locally driven success story, reviving this iconic block and gradually restoring it to its past glory.

Let's not forget that Hastings is still a seaside resort well worth visiting too. It has a wonderfully quirky Old Town and

Castle dating back to King William's time (that William, victor at that battle) and was one of the Cinque ports in the twelfth century. But a quick scamper through the town's thousand-year history confirms the view that this is a place that has had to ride a whole series of ups and downs. All this contributes to the feeling that we have here a strangely quirky, chaotic and at times, anarchic town.

Where concrete calmed the storms

As a possible sign of things to come, Hastings suffered badly from storms and flooding in the thirteenth century and raids and attacks from the French in the fourteenth century. The port and town went into a steady decline only to be rescued by emerging as a seaside resort after the Napoleonic Wars.

Elegant crescents of houses were built out of the narrow valley of the Bourne stream where the Old Town with its ancient houses and tiny alleys or 'twittens' sat. This growth eventually linked up with the new Regency resort of St Leonards, which itself owed its development from 1826 onwards to James Burton, a London property developer and his son, Decimus Burton.

It was at this time that the itinerant builders and workforce needed to construct the properties settled in a small area by the town, which became known as the America Ground. This grew to cover about eight acres, housing 1,000 people. The whole area acquired an anarchic reputation as a den of iniquity with some homes just half-sawn boats stuck on end, but many commentators view it as a thriving libertarian self-contained community. The name emerged from a revolt in the 1800s when bailiffs were chased out and the American flag was raised as a sign of the place asserting its 'independence'.

In 1835 wholesale evictions took place with many residents moving on to St Leonards. It lay derelict for fourteen years before being developed as part of an expanding town. Even today the streets of Robertson Street, Carlisle Parade and Robertson Terrace are still known as the America Ground.

By the turn of the twentieth century Hastings had its elegant and expensive terraces and squares alongside growing poverty and poor-quality housing crammed into its valleys. You get a feel for the town at this time from the author Robert Tressell who wrote *The Ragged Trousered Philanthropist* in 1914. He based his description of Mugsborough on Hastings after moving to the town in 1901, centring his book on those he worked alongside whilst living in Hastings.

In the Edwardian era, Hastings as a resort went into decline in comparison with its posher neighbour, St Leonards. In response, the local Council sought inspiration from a new Borough Engineer who was prepared to think big. A huge investment in the town's seafront development owed much to the arrival of Sidney Little, known as the 'Concrete King', who became the council's chosen engineer in the 1930s. As the soubriquet suggests, Sidney Little had a love of reinforced concrete. He put it to use on the seafront designing the first underground car-park in the country, a huge open air swimming pool (that struggled for viability and was closed in 1986 and in typical Hastings fashion lay vacant for thirty years), modernist concrete shelters and a vast double-decked concrete promenade that produced a covered walkway decorated with fragments of bottles. This quickly acquired the nickname 'Bottle Alley' and for many years was the home of the town's homeless and drinkers. It now hosts a dramatic light display and has been extensively cleaned up. I strolled through it on a sunny day and despite this work I have to say it still felt a bit threatening and claustrophobic.

The investment in the Bottle Alley promenade ably sums up the overall issues facing Hastings. Is the light show just lipstick on a pig? Is Hastings going to be relentlessly damned by short term cash injections, mis-managed by both public and private agencies constantly living in a dream world where gentrification is going to overcome the resolutely deep and structural problems of poverty in the town.

In 2019, the Government indices for deprivation showed that only twelve boroughs in the country had worse scores than Hastings, across a range of measures including employment, education, crime and barriers to housing. In eleven areas these measures had actually got worse since the previous publication. At the same time, gentrification and the arrival of the 'DFL's' (down from London) or the less pleasing 'FILTH' (failed in London, try Hastings) has brought in the quirky art galleries, trendy shops, artist studios and independent cafés. These sit happily amongst the long-standing eclectic retail offers in George Street and High Street.

The future remains uncertain for the town as investment ebbs and flows. The eclectic vitality of the shopping area contrasts with the poor state of many buildings and the grotty lumps from the 1960s and 1970s interspersed with cash injections into older homes and cottages. The social and community enterprises fight for funding, assets and support whilst the economy continues to frustrate investment at a level sufficient to tackle the deep-seated structural problems that have been around since Robert Tressell's day. Local people are trying to get a grip themselves and all power to them. In the meantime, go down to the seafront, visit the Pier, the Old Town shops and the Contemporary, pop into the Source and walk along Sidney Little's concrete promenade. It's worth it.

CHAPTER TWELVE

Weymouth and Weston-super-Mare: lost opportunities by the finest of bays

*Weymouth is a sweet, clean and agreeable town,
considering its low location and close to the sea*

Daniel Defoe, who visited in the 1720s

*If a stranger first enters it on a stormy day and at low water,
he may perhaps feel inclined to turn his horses.*

Guidebook to Weston-super-Mare in 1822

Two seaside resorts on giant sweeps of sand. To Weymouth on the south coast and Weston-super-Mare facing Wales across the Bristol Channel. Very different histories but both facing the same problems over investment and how best to take the opportunities each clearly has in terms of environment and geography.

It wasn't just Daniel Defoe who took a liking to Weymouth. The town owes much of its early success to King George III who liked it so much he spent summers taking in the sea air whilst staying with his brother on the seafront. More recently Paul Theroux, the writer and travel fan, on his mostly unhappy tour of Britain's coast in *A Kingdom by the Sea,* waxed lyrical about the place. 'It was grand without being pompous' he said. 'It had a real harbour. It was full of boats. All its architecture was intact, the late-Georgian terraces facing the Esplanade and the sea, and cottages and old warehouses on the harbour'. He even felt he could live here.

Lots of people agree. *Country Living* magazine, essential reading for the footloose lover of the best of Britain, named Weymouth as the second-best place to live by the sea in 2021, after a rejuvenated Margate. Second homeowners are moving in with the *Dorset Echo* reporting that in 2018 alone one quarter of all house sales in the town went to second homeowners. Even the *Rough Guide* with its more eclectic choices, regards it as one of the best seaside resorts in the UK. And why not? It has one of the country's finest sweeps of beach sitting amidst the Jurassic World Heritage coastline, a busy and bustling harbour surrounded by those Theroux-loved Georgian terraces, lots of sunshine hours, excellent countryside around it and a seaside history with forts and castles, all brought bang up to date by the arrival of the sailing Olympics in 2012.

The readers of *Which?* in 2020 seemed to agree, giving four stars to the beach, the seafront, the scenery and attractions. They were less enamoured with the peace and quiet and shopping on offer, perhaps symptomatic of a town which needs lots of new retail investment, whilst busily being promoted on activity websites as *Las Weygas,* the new 'hen and stag' capital of the UK.

Trouble is, has Weymouth really taken advantage of all these great opportunities? Sure, the place is busy and bustling in the summer season and it has its fair share of festivals and attractions to draw folk into the town. But as a visitor, knowing a little of the past of the town, I can't help feeling that Weymouth lacks the feel you get from places like Hastings or Folkestone that have sought to embrace either the personal entrepreneurship of philanthropists or the verve and dynamism of a vibrant local community spirit. It also suffers from some frankly awful architectural lumps such as the Cineworld, TKMax and Range retail and leisure centres facing the marina on the enticingly named Commercial Road as well as the concrete decay of the old Council offices on North Quay. The place is growing though, with new housing developments spreading out into the countryside and retail parks grabbing land around its much-needed relief roads that circle the town. Whither Weymouth, is the question I must ask?

Brand Weymouth is a work in progress. Its hugely positive side revolves around an exceptional history, environment, harbour and a series of innovative schemes that are rejuvenating parts of the town and its sailing legacy. On the flip side are the perennial problems of many seaside towns: the instability of investment, the uncertainty about what type of future activity the town needs or desires and a prevaricating set of decision makers unable to settle on what is best for the future. Let's look at the two sides of Weymouth today and begin with its fascinating history.

> *The boats, the sands, the esplanade,*
> *The laughing crowd;*
> *Light-hearted, loud*
> *Greetings from some not ill-endowed*

The lines above come from a poem entitled 'At a seaside

town in 1869 (young lovers reverie)' by Thomas Hardy, a man who mixed the familiar with made up places and who certainly used Weymouth as an inspiration in some of his work. Today, it still captures the vibrancy of the Weymouth seafront and beach. Weymouth has been a draw for tourists of all kinds since it was first popularised by the visits of King George III in the late 1700s.

The town has a history built around its resort and port growth over three centuries. It was once two small towns, Melcombe Regis to the north-east of the small Wey River mouth and Weymouth to the south-west. It is said that the port of Melcombe Regis saw the arrival of the Black Death in England in 1348. The two had a history of disputes and rivalries as port towns until an Act of Union by Elizabeth I brought them together in 1571 and it took until 1597 for the two ports to be connected by a bridge.

As the single port of Weymouth, the town witnessed a series of tumultuous events including the sending of twenty ships to fight in the Spanish Armada, the departure of many pilgrims to the new world of America and two battles during the Civil War. Weymouth still has a reminder of those battles in 1645; a cannonball is firmly lodged in a house on the corner of Maiden Street and St Edmund Street.

It wasn't until the mid-1700s that its success as a resort town took off. English Heritage reported the first reference to sea-bathing in 1748 with a request to install two 'bathing houses' by the harbour. A wealthy Bath resident, Ralph Allen, took a shine to the town and built a house on the Esplanade which still stands today. He used his royal connections to persuade a sickly George III to visit in 1789 enjoying the spa waters of local wells (that are said to have first cured local sheep) and the sea air. He stayed for ten weeks in his brother's house at Gloucester Lodge (which he eventually bought) and as they say, the rest is history.

The royal patronage right up to 1805 brought the wealthy to the town, bringing expensive new developments and facilities, including bathing huts on wheels, a Library (offering rather more than just books and now a seafront nightclub), Assembly Rooms, (now the Old Rooms Inn) and one of the first purpose-built theatres outside London.

All along the Esplanade are names associated with royalty of the time and the grateful residents of the town raised public funds in 1810 to mark the King's Golden Jubilee with a very grand and colourful statue of him. He got another local thank you in 1808 with the carving of the King on a horse cut into the chalk hillside above Osmington near the town.

Rise and fall

Up to the arrival of the railway in 1857 Weymouth remained a resort of privilege but thereafter, in common with many seaside resorts, it opened up to a newly mobile, more work-ing-class visitor. A different range of activities became popular with donkey rides, Punch and Judy and the town's unique sand sculptures. A working pier, built in 1933 had two railway tracks to bring passengers directly to boats ready to sail off to the Channel Islands but the rail link shut down in the early 1990s.

One major addition to the seafront in the twentieth century was the Pavilion Theatre. The Pavilion and indeed the whole pier area around it, is a classic example of Weymouth messing up its opportunities. Originally built in 1908, it burnt down in 1954 and was rebuilt in 1960 as a rather ugly lump with blank walls facing three sides of the harbour around it. It still dominates the seafront and the entrance to the Peninsula site and has become a classic symbol of the prevarication over the direction of Weymouth as a resort. Whilst it continues to offer its motley collection of tribute acts, live music, opera and comedians its future depends on the success of the community interest company that took it over in 2013.

By 2000 the Council had started to worry about its future as a part of one of Weymouth's longest lasting regeneration plans, the redevelopment of the whole Pier peninsula. In 2005 the Pavilion was closed awaiting its inclusion in the new scheme, only for the proposed developer to go bankrupt in 2009. The Pavilion limped on to 2012 when after a temporary respite during the Olympics, once again a plan emerged to demolish it. The local fight back began and in 2013, led by a local businessman, it reopened as a community interest company and doubled visitor numbers in just one year. The Covid inspired lockdown in 2020 hit the Pavilion heavily but a grant from the Government's Culture Recovery Fund rescued its finances and it powers on today.

The Pier peninsula site, on which the Pavilion sits, is currently a vast car-park, deserted by Condor Ferries whilst the search continues for new investment in a scheme worthy of its fabulous location. Masterplans for the site came and went, planning permissions were granted by the Council for mixed use entertainment facilities and new homes, but no developer bought into the dream for the future. The site was cleared and a temporary but dramatic fifty-three metre observation tower, known as the Jurassic Skyline, opened in time for the Olympics on the site. In 2017 several visitors had to be air-lifted from its stuck lift. It couldn't be repaired and bang... down it came. A single sign pointing to the Tower, by the equally sad looking entrance to the 'Pleasure Pier', is the only reminder of its past glory.

Today the site's future hangs in the balance. With Condor unlikely to return and a post-Covid investment market uncertain about the viability of any future plans, it sits there, throbbing gently away, a busy but desolate car-park sticking out into the sea.

Body blows to Weymouth

Weymouth has got lots of potential and has had its chances. There is no doubt that the loss of around 4,500 jobs and income of £40 million a year when the Navy left Portland in 1995 was a huge blow to a town lacking anything so dominant to take the strain.

Weymouth and Portland have been strategically important to the defence of the country since Roman times and King Henry VIII had two castles built at Portland and Sandsfoot to protect the harbour. The breakwaters across the harbour were completed by the end of the 1860s and since then the Royal Navy gradually stepped up its presence in Portland. Despite playing a key role in both World Wars and being heavily bombed by the Germans anxious to wipe out its facilities, it was the end of the Cold War that brought the biggest changes to the port. A review of Navy services proposed closure in 1992 and despite local opposition, three years later the Navy left for good.

The port facilities were privately purchased in 1996 and as a commercial operation it continues to be busy and thriving, handling all manner of private vessels as well as offering a terminal for cruise ships. The site of the old Navy Air Station base has been redeveloped and renamed Osprey Quay under the management of the Land Trust, a national land management charity. It now hosts a variety of industrial, retail, leisure and residential uses, the largest new marina on the south coast and the new Sailing Academy, bringing much-needed regeneration to the area.

Despite all this new investment, nothing the size of the Navy establishment has returned. Portland's own Neighbourhood Plan points out that of 300 businesses on the 'island' (as it's known), only ten employ more than 50 people. Thomas Hardy described the island as 'the peninsula carved by time from a single stone' and its past and current quarrying industry still pock-marks the strange local environment. Portland has long been famous for the quality of its stone and Sir Christopher Wren, who was the MP for Weymouth in 1702, used it for many of his architectural masterpieces including St Paul's Cathedral. Scattered terraced villages separated by windswept quarries and tree-less fields with the ever-present coastline never far away, mark Portland out as a very different place to its tourist-thronged neighbour.

Sadly, an attempt to draw visitors into an old quarry on the island with a dinosaur themed museum known as *Jurassica,* fell apart in 2017. Despite having the entrepreneurial Tim Smit of the Eden Project in Cornwall on the board, it struggled to raise money. A decision was taken to merge the project with another scheme known as *The Journey*, to promote biodiversity in a disused mine. By 2018 *The Journey* had morphed into *Eden Portland*, in an attempt to benefit from Tim Smit's well-known brand. The project's website doesn't hold back, hyping up the hole in the ground as 'a theatre of science like nowhere else; a space in which to explore the importance of biodiversity, the threat of extinction and what it means to be human'. Today it is still an idea, rather than something physical to draw tourists over to Portland. Yet another of those coastal investment projects that struggles for life.

Over in Weymouth, the loss of the Condor Ferry service in 2015 was only meant to be a temporary blow but seems to have turned into a permanent change taking both jobs and the vibrancy of an active continental port away from Weymouth. The size of the new ferries, the deteriorating state of the sea walls and a lack of council funding for repairs meant that Condor left Weymouth in 2015. Despite a wish for the company to return to bring a buzz and business back to Weymouth, it is now unlikely to happen and the Council is left with a valuable piece of empty coastal real estate. It still has the old railway lines in place where the trains ran to connect to ferries, but little else to mark a vibrant history of passenger traffic.

Elsewhere in the town the need for fresh investment and long-term commitment is easy to spot in the streets behind Weymouth's bustling Esplanade and the harbour-facing Custom House Quay. Development plans for new housing and hotels abound for back street sites like the old Bowling Alley on St Nicholas Street or School Street Plaza, a small indoor shopping centre empty since 2019 and the concrete lump of the old Council offices across the harbour on North Quay, empty since 2016. Apart from the iconic seaside location of the Peninsula there is also the twelve-acre site on the waterfront at Newtons Cove where the old QinetiQ Bincleaves technology park once sat. Now proposed as another residential and hotel site, it too has sat vacant for years as proposals for a care village failed to proceed.

Further south is Sandsfoot Castle, yet another of Henry VIII's defensive forts, dating from 1542 but now in ruins and under severe threat of collapsing into the sea. The owners, the County Council, don't seem to have the resources to underpin the cliff on which it sits and the Castle currently has an uncertain future despite huge local support for it to be saved.

On the Westwey Road, on the west side of the Marina, sits the site of the old eyesore of a now demolished gas holder and the depot of Southern Electric, two more sites that need proposals for development to get going. There is also an uncertain future for the well-loved Brewers Quay, south of the harbour, after a proposal to convert it to luxury homes fell through, followed by a further failure to take it on as a community owned asset by the local Development Trust.

All in all, a lot of money is needed to restore or regenerate so many of Weymouth's prime sites.

An Olympian legacy?

The arrival of the sailing teams for the Olympics in 2012 could have helped to reverse a downward spiral that had taken central parts of Weymouth and Portland into the top ten per cent for levels of deprivation. In 2019 the *Dorset Echo* was reporting that a local conference on poverty in the area had highlighted the fact that around 40% of children in parts of the town were living in poverty. The Child Poverty Action Group classifies children as living in poverty if their families are living on benefits or working tax credits and their income is less than 60% of the working median.

Five years earlier things were no better. *The Guardian* reported a local charity worker quoting the town as 'a prison of passion, a graveyard of ambition' and recommending young people get out of town for a better future. The Deputy Principal of the local college commented on Weymouth being a lovely place to live but without a car it was extremely difficult to get around compounding the sense of rural isolation in this part of Dorset.

Weymouth is a resort stuffed with history and its elegant Esplanade, Georgian terraces, fine beach and boat-studded harbour presented the perfect sailing base for the 2012 Olympics. The choice of the town (with Portland) as a base for sailing brought in, according to local reports, over £177 millions of infrastructure, bus and rail improvements and regeneration projects, not to mention the appearance of the strange floating rocks at the oddly named Jurassic roundabout, as you drive into town. Here was an opportunity for Weymouth and Portland to give their economies, infrastructure and finances a real long-lasting boost and hopefully a long-term legacy.

Not everyone was happy though. As I mentioned earlier visitor numbers didn't meet expectations despite 80,000 visitors hitting the beach on one sailing day. Local retailers and hoteliers seemed to believe that the sheer hype around the Games actually put the more traditional visitors off and after all, sailing isn't the easiest sport to watch from land. The Bayside

Festival on the Pavilion peninsula had to close after two weeks due to poor numbers and local residents didn't take kindly to a prime viewing spot by Nothe Castle being turned into a ticket-only spot.

Even much welcomed investment exacerbated long held enmities between the two neighbours, Weymouth and Portland. The Olympics did bring a £6m investment in the Weymouth and Portland National Sailing Academy, as part of a huge regeneration project designed to transform the old Navy base on Portland. In 2008, Portlanders reportedly took umbrage that Weymouth had laid a claim to the regenerated parts of Portland becoming a part of Weymouth for promotional purposes. Apart from the Academy, marina and the Portland stone Olympic ring sculpture above Fortuneswell, much of the regeneration money passed Portland by. Even today, just up the hill from the marina in Fortuneswell, levels of deprivation are the worst in the area and any visitor can see the stark contrast between the bustle and resort-led vibrancy of Weymouth over the more post-industrial and quarry-scarred environment of Portland.

In 2013 the House of Lords Olympic Legacy Committee reported that it felt that the opportunity to promote Weymouth and Portland after the Games had been missed by a 'London-centric' approach that ignored chances to fund new initiatives in the town.

On the flip side the Games really raised the national and international profile of Weymouth. The beach was free to use and huge TV screens beamed the distant action to viewers. Cruise ship numbers increased, attracted to the port as an opportunity for day visits to Dorset or the town, with a reported sixty-two due to moor up off the resort in the 2022 cruising season. To be honest it's probably the post-Covid burst of UK based holidays that has really saved Weymouth. The 2022 summer, long and hot as it was, brought the crowds in and filled the fish and chip shops.

The legacy of the Olympics is still a matter of debate in the town. Huge preparatory expenditure on the town's chronic road access brought a relief road and intelligent traffic lighting as well as, rather late in the day, an improved broadband system. Projections of over 850,000 visitors to the sailing events failed to materialise with just over 50% of the estimate being achieved. The type of visitor wasn't the traditional Weymouth tourist either. Comments were made to local press about the sailing aficionados being a different bunch to the more beach and entertainment orientated families who may even have been put off by the tales of difficult road journeys and sailing not being their thing.

A classic difference in the direction of a future Weymouth was there for all to see. How best was Weymouth to use its undoubted advantages as a seaside resort; go upmarket with offers of high-quality sailing and top hotels or continue to cater for a more family-based set of traditional activities. Go posh or go bucket and spade? Weymouth struggled to find its place after the Olympics and today, busy as it is, it still struggles.

It was perhaps no surprise then to find that in 2022 the local council turned to that doyen of seaside regeneration, Wayne Hemingway (remember him from Hunstanton and Exmouth) to come up with the ideas past proposals had failed to bring to the resort. Once again Hemingway talked of the 'potential' and need for 'evolution' before spending the council's money on yet another local consultation exercise. Presumably more food options, hotels and attractions would be mooted by the king of seaside consulting.

Whither Weymouth?

The crowds may have returned but there is no doubt that Weymouth could benefit from some more long-lasting investment that goes beyond the cheaper fish and chips and bucket and spade driven end of the economy. Its appeal revolves around the seafront Esplanade and harbour areas where attractive buildings and vibrant cafes, restaurants, shops, hotels and seaside attractions are clearly most successful. The pedestrianised shopping streets tucked in behind these waterfront streets provide Weymouth with its more varied shopping experience but to be honest, add little more to the towns character.

You couldn't say the town was a discreet and peaceful seaside spot. It is as raucous as Skegness at times and the bars spilling youngsters into the harbour side streets were pounding with music and the smell of chips on a summer's day. That's what the towns renowned live music scene offers along with a reputation for stag and hen parties. So that's what you get in certain parts of the town. There are more peaceful spots over by the Nothe with its park and waterfront paths and the waterside walks in all directions are the perfect counterpoint to the busy harbour and Esplanade.

So whither Weymouth? As one local member of the community action group *Weyprogress* put it back in April 2019, 'vision, creativity and daring to be different are the qualities that transform places and the lives of people who live there. Too often our local politicians and council officers take what seems to them to be the safe option, but in reality it is the riskiest, because it is too safe, boring and ill-conceived to make the impact necessary to rebuild local confidence and energy levels'. Well said. Given these views you can understand why Wayne Hemingway was invited in and asked to develop some fresh and innovative proposals to rejuvenate the seafront. He really is the go-to man if you have run out of ideas. This could apply to so many of our seaside towns but certainly Weymouth faces a particular challenge given the opportunities it has in terms of waterside land and investment attractions. Unfortunately Hemingway's ideas have not gone down well, as Councillors in January 2023 accused him of going 'off script' and ignoring what local people wanted. Oh dear. Weymouth has to think again, again.

The wrong weather for Weston-super-Mare

The quote from the 1822 Guidebook to Weston-super-Mare at the start of this chapter didn't hold back in expressing the view that poor weather and a low tide might discourage visitors. Two hundred years on, I'm sorry to say, the Guidebook is right. I did feel inclined to turn my proverbial horses as the rain teemed down, the sea had long disappeared over the horizon and Weston-super-Mud, as it's known locally when the tide is out, offered me its dreariest and most depressing face.

The rain had arrived after a long hot summer, totally catching out the wandering visitors on the seafront, still clad in their now sopping wet T-shirts and soggy flip-flops. As the increasingly desperate families dived for cover in steaming cafes or shelter under the pier, I fought my way up the seafront, past the sad donkeys, to 'enjoy' the resorts attractions.

Top of my list was the latest draw to the resort of Weston, the See Monster, a huge oil rig decommissioned from the North Sea, transplanted onto the beach behind the old Tropicana. It was closed. Even the viewing platform was closed. I could see it of course, lurking behind two cranes looking like… a decommissioned oil rig dumped on to the beach, straight out of the North Sea. In full use for just eight weeks at an estimated cost of £10.5 million it was the most expensive of the generally unloved and unheralded Unboxed festival schemes dreamt up to supposedly show off British ingenuity post-Brexit.

The Tropicana itself has lost the obvious allure it had in the past. For 63 years from its opening in 1937, it had offered Weston a huge open-air swimming pool that attracted the likes of Haile Selassie, when he lived in Bath between 1936 and 1940 and evidently Diana Dors, who came third in the beauty Queen competition here in 1945. Now it is the Bay Café and for five weeks in 2015 it flourished as perhaps Weston's most famous (or infamous) attraction, *Dismaland*, an ironic mickey-taking attraction by the notorious artist Banksy. Designed as a 'sinister twist on Disneyland' it brought in over 150,000 visitors and £20 million to the town after its highly secretive arrival. It was full of scandalous stuff from 58 different designers and artists. The public loved it. If only it could have stayed, but then that wouldn't have been what Banksy wanted.

All hail Weston College

I think the *Which?* visitors turned up in the rain too. They didn't like the peace and quiet, value for money, food and drink or shopping on offer and dumped Weston into the bottom group of scored resorts. By 2022 *Which?* had dumped it even further down the list, sitting just above Skegness. To be honest the shopping is pretty bleak with the Sovereign retail centre clearly under the weather (so to speak) with a leaky ceiling, empty units and the desolate repetitiveness of every other shopping centre in the country.

Evidently the local council bought it for a sum now five times its current value and has 'ambitious' plans for its revival with new workspaces for those much sought-after 'creative' types. The Sovereign throws you out into the 'Italian Gardens' which are not really Italian or a garden. There are small fountains though for wet kids to get wetter in.

Across from the 'Gardens' is the Winter Gardens, opened in 1927, a low-slung ballroom that became a base for the BBC during the Blitz. From the 1950s to the 1970s it hosted many top music acts but as competition grew from bigger halls the future looked bleak. By the early 1980s the local council was even considering demolition but investment at the end of the decade saw it grow into a conference facility that was heavily used by the local Weston College. The College's use expanded and by 2015 the council agreed to pass ownership of the whole building to the College. A £15 million programme of refurbishment saw the building revitalised as an educational centre with further spend on the ballroom, restaurant and reception.

There is no doubt that Weston College plays an important role in the town today. Rated as one of the best colleges in the UK supporting over 30,000 learners it provides further and higher education to all those over 14. As one of the top ten colleges in size in the country, it is a major employer in the town with over 500 staff. Its role has expanded over time into offender learning, events and restaurant management, conference facilities and special education needs and its links to two universities have led to the local PR merchants dubbing Weston a 'university town'.

Stemming the drugs tide

Weston certainly needs Weston College. Like many of the seaside resorts we have visited it has its acute poverty issues. The Office for National Statistics reported in 2017 that nearly 40% of families were living in poverty, with stark differences between wealthier suburban and poorer central parts of the town.

The large Victorian terraces and mansions that once housed the wealthier visitors to the town have now been broken up into a huge range of rented or cheaper flats of varying quality, housing many poorer families and single people. Where houses have been retained as single homes a different kind of use crept quietly into the town. By the turn of the century Weston slowly became the drug and rehabilitation centre of England as landlords used bedsits to house addicts and larger good value houses became rehabilitation centres. Residents of so-called dry houses (where recovering addicts lived alone), outside of the social care inspection regime, began to get the blame for local crime rising and the Council decided it was time to act. An accreditation scheme was brought in to try and regulate what had become, by 2006, the home of 11% of all the drug rehabilitation beds in the country, regulated and unregulated.

The regulation scheme seemed to do the trick. By 2012 *The Guardian* was reporting that the number of beds had dropped to 262 against 500 six years earlier and a more professional and well-run service was on offer. It's less of a discussion point now in the town but there are still drug raids and closure orders (where the police close down a house used for drugs) appearing in the local press. It seems it's hard for Weston to throw off its past problems entirely.

Tale of two Piers

Long before drug rehab, See Monsters and Weston College, at the start of the 19th century, Weston was just a small village of thirty houses behind a range of sand dunes. Much of the local area was owned by the Smyth-Pigotts, whose land extended from Weston right across to Bristol. In common with many early resorts, it was the promise of sea-bathing promoted by local doctors that brought the gentry in and Knightstone Island, just by the seafront marina still has a Georgian bath-house built in 1832.

Once again it was the arrival of the railway, this time in 1841, that was to transform the place into a bustling resort. The railway wasn't universally welcomed. Residents fought to push the station away, so it was built some distance from the centre on the main line to Exeter. Passengers were then ferried along a branch line into town by horse drawn carriages. The site of the final station at that time is now a well-kept floral display on Regent Street, with a scaled down replica steam engine similar to the one that first ran on the stretch of line from Exeter standing forlornly by.

New terraces and villa developments, built in local stone and dressed in Bath limestone, quickly spread to Royal Crescent, Landemann Circus and Grove Park and are still some of

Weston's finest buildings today. *Historic England* reported that Weston attracted many notable engineers and architects including Joseph Bazelgette, the man who designed both London and Weston's sewer system and Hans Price who designed many of the town's buildings from 1860 to 1912.

Paddle steamers from Wales could also land at the new Birnbeck Pier by 1867 with the local Weston Museum reporting that 120,000 people paid a one penny admission on the pier in the first three months. Designed by Eugenius Birch it was unique in linking the mainland to an island.

The Birnbeck Pier's position did little for the growing centre of town however and by the late 1800s money was being raised locally for a new pier. It took until 1904 for the first section of the Grand Pier to open with an end of Pier entertainment venue. An attempt was made to extend it for seafaring traffic in 1907 but the huge tidal range of the Bristol Channel defeated regular moorings and it was dismantled. Today it's a very busy central attraction, but do they really need to charge £1 to walk along it? I suppose that, as the pier Pavilion burnt down in 2008 and it cost over £50 million to restore it, the money must be recouped somehow.

The Birnbeck Pier needs even more money. It is isolated away from the town, on the Worlebury headland, away from the helter-skelter of the town beach. It is Grade II* listed but suffering badly. After seeing duty as a weapons testing facility in the War, seafaring visiting declined and ended in 1979. Ownerships and proposals for its future came and went including a four-year ownership by housing regeneration specialists *Urban Splash*. Eventually, tiring of the increasing dereliction and inaction by the then owner *CNN Estates,* the Council bought the pier in 2021. Once again proposals from the Council, the RNLI and Historic England emerged but little is happening at present to save the pier.

It wasn't just the railway and the boats that brought visitors to Weston. In 1936 the town acquired an airfield, an ambitious gamble by the Council to put the town on the aviation map. For a while it certainly worked, with 20,000 passengers a year coming in from Wales, Birmingham and France. Public use of the airfield ceased in 2012 but it still houses the Helicopter Museum, a reminder of Weston's days as the home of Westland Helicopters.

What are your wishes for Weston?

Weston is a growing town with new housing and industrial parks spreading out to the M5, but it also needs fresh investment in the core of the resort. Not just for the Birnbeck Pier but also to fill the cleared sites in the town centre with vibrant new uses, the revitalising of the Sovereign Centre and the reuse of several empty and decaying shops. I liked the great little Weston Museum and an outbreak of vivid colourful street art has filled a lot of blank walls. Investment in the public spaces on the seafront has smartened the esplanade up too.

Sadly, not every addition has been fully welcomed by the good people of Weston. The curious thirty-metre-high *Silica* sculpture-come rain shelter in the town centre is a love me-hate me object that struck me as something whipped off the top of a Burmese pagoda. Locals call it *The Carrot*. A plaintive sign on the side of one empty shop, obviously last used as a temporary information point to draw in views of the town, pleads 'what are your wishes for Weston?' Less rain for a start, and more action to speed the revival of Weston.

When asked the question 'what should Weston be famous for' when responding to the Councils prospectus for change, local people knew that this was a resort for leisure, first and foremost. But it needs an upgrade. Aged and decaying Victoriana, (think Birnbeck Pier, the Tropicana and empty shops) do nothing to attract new money or new business. Repeated phrases like 'downmarket', a 'lack of cultural variety', 'be bold' and 'a need for variety and vibrancy' were meshed in with a love for the towns Victorian character. Weston folk are right but getting all this sorted in these times where so many seaside resorts are competing for the long-term investment god of regeneration and revival will be a tough one.

And what of that name too. How come Weston is a 'super-Mare'? It's simple enough it seems. Weston was so common a name in this area in medieval times that it was given the Latin addition to distinguish it; *super mare* being 'above sea'. Time to make Weston super again.

CHAPTER THIRTEEN

Newquay and St Mawes: surf's up and so are prices

'Where is the best restaurant in Newquay and will they take a stag party of thirty?'

A recent TripAdvisor enquiry

'As they arrive, the lopsided, unjust housing system marches local families out to a precarious existence in the crammed estates of inland towns'

A quote from an ex-MP on what is happening to the housing market as second homeowners arrive in places like St Mawes

To Newquay, the surfing capital of the UK, the home of stag and hen parties, far too many homeless people for a town of its size and host to the newest Spaceport in the country. Spaceport? It seems Newquay is a town of curious contrasts. Full of tourists loving its wonderful beaches, bleached surfers riding the country's best waves and big gangs of stag and hen parties looking for booze and laughs. Oh, and a pair of Duchy of Cornwall inspired sustainable housing estates designed to embody the principles of architecture and urban planning of the new King Charles III, topped off with an amazing attempt to bring to Cornwall the world's most environmentally friendly launch location for satellites. All this alongside a real housing crisis as desperate local people are turfed out of homes, when better returns can be made from temporarily visiting families, and rough sleepers seek out a warmer base to camp out.

Contrasts and dilemmas

A town of contrasts indeed. In the summer it can attract over 100,000 visitors a day, five times its current population. Its beaches are renowned for their beauty, waves and safety. It holds a quarter of all of Cornwall's bedspaces for visitors, but this holiday seasonality brings the traditional seaside resort problems of low wages, irregular work and housing shortages compounded by the town's inaccessibility. Our guides, the readers of *Which?* found it to be a place of contrasts too, awarding the resort high marks for the beaches and scenery but poor scores for peace and quiet, shopping and value for money.

As one of Cornwall's biggest towns, Newquay is a popular place to live and the growing town is facing up to the need to regenerate and modernise in an increasingly competitive world for tourism. This has brought its own stresses and strains as massive new investments are proposed and brought to the town, often in the teeth of local concerns and disquiet over what Newquay has become, or will become.

Back in the fifteenth century the town was a small fishing village known by its old Cornish name of Towan Blystra. It acquired its new name after a new quay was built by funds raised by the Bishop of Exeter in the mid 1400s. By 1835 a stone harbour had been constructed and the town began a boom period from fishing, tin mining and agriculture. Newquay became famous for its pilchard catch in the eighteenth century and it still has the huer's hut up on the cliff which was used as a lookout post by the 'huer' who put out the call to fishermen when pilchard shoals were spotted offshore.

In 1876 the railway arrived bringing a different kind of shoal: tourists. This led to the opening up of the first purpose-built hotel, the Great Western, in 1879, designed by one of Cornwall's first hotel architects and entrepreneurs, Silvanus Trevail. In 1900 the huge Headland Hotel was completed by Trevail on the cliff above the Fistral beach. Deliberately built as the supposed best hotel in the south-west, its development upset the local fishermen who dried their nets on what they considered to be common land. Attacks on the foundations turned into what became known as the Newquay riots, involving hundreds of local people, forcing the construction work to stop. This was to be the first sign of how Newquay was changing from a rough and ready fishing and port village into a higher-class tourist spot and the locals didn't all welcome the change.

Trevail had also added the Atlantic Hotel to his design portfolio further round the headland near the Huer's Hut in 1892. Its claim to fame really came in 1967 when the Beatles stayed for three nights on their *Magical Mystery Tour*, bringing Beatlemania hysteria to the town.

Newquay has had its hotel ups and downs. The Fistral Bay Hotel, empty for fifteen years, is finally to be turned into new housing after years of inaction and failed proposals. Cliffdene Hotel, the La Felica, Fort Wayne, Kelsbro, Trebarwith,

Edgcumbe, St Brannocks and Tolcarne hotels have all closed their doors as a result of the declining popularity of their old-fashioned holiday offer. Even now, as staycations boom once again and the resort is filled with tourists, fresh proposals for the redevelopment of two of Newquay's cliff top hotels, the Narrowcliff and the Bristol, dominate local headlines. A scheme to build a new hotel, restaurants and 177 flats of up to fourteen storeys has been greeted with local alarm as residents object to what they describe as a 'hideous monstrosity'.

The scheme encapsulates a dilemma for Newquay. Do you bring in huge investment to capitalise on the need for high quality hotels, housing, retail and leisure facilities or fight off the 'wrong sort' of development in an undoubted popular and beautiful location? How best to meet the demands of a visiting population, whilst dealing with the traditional seaside resort problems of low wages, insecure housing and seasonality? In Newquay these issues have been compounded by the town not always attracting the 'right sort of tourist' in the past, whether it be stags and hens, rough sleepers or 'van-lifers', living out their lives in the town's streets and car parks. All mixed in with thousands of families enjoying the wonderful beaches and local attractions.

Out with the mankini

Newquay has had some odd little battles in the past as it has tried to deal with a few unwanted problems thrown up by its popularity, reputation and a common set of seaside resort issues.

In 2009 many Newquay locals had had enough of their

town's reputation as a hardcore party resort for under-age kids keen on drink and parties. It had become a post-exam pilgrimage for youngsters camping out alongside marauding stags and hens who quickly turned the town centre into an unfriendly place after dark. A dramatic event was to be the catalyst for change. Two teenagers died falling from the cliffs and a third was seriously injured just a few days apart. The local residents had had enough. 3,000 signatures were collected and many residents marched through the town demanding action from the police and council and seeking a change to what seemed to be a permissive culture of bad behaviour.

A fresh approach, called Newquay Safe, built around a partnership of local people, the council, police, businesses and drug and alcohol agencies, began to tackle the drivers of the behaviour in the town. Lap-dancing clubs, seen as hosts to much bad behaviour, were heavily licensed and many closed. Under-age controls on drinking were enforced. Parents were contacted and asked to take home under-age children found drunk. Drink was confiscated in the street. Even what people wore around the town became the subject of tight controls. Tackling the town's reputation as a party haven saw a ban on 'mankini's', the tiny, strange swimming trunks made popular by Sacha Baron Cohen in his film *Borat*. Wearing offensive T-shirts or carrying inflatable genitalia was banned in pubs and venues.

Local people saw a lot of change in the years that followed, supported by a move to grow surfing and its associated businesses in the town, a more up-market set of shops, cafes and restaurants and a set of family-orientated attractions. Everything has not completely changed though. Just a few years ago *The Mirror* newspaper dubbed the town *Magaluf UK* and a 'shrine to debauchery' as it reported on gangs of young drunk men and women rolling through the streets. If they were too young to get into bars they drank on the beaches. One local commented that the town was full of 'over-qualified babysitters' catering for the needs of raucous young drunk kids. 'If you are not a cabbie, a bouncer, a policeman, a surfing instructor or you work in a kebab shop, there is no work' he said.

Damning stuff indeed and evidence that Newquay has not completely shaken off its party past. But the comments about the problems of work in the town seemed to be underlined by the Government's own statistics. The Newquay Central ward, centred on the streets close to Narrowcliff, had shown in 2017 that the area was one of the most deprived in Cornwall and in the ten per cent most deprived in the country. And things were getting worse. Not seven years earlier this area had not been in the worse twenty per cent. Worsening levels of crime, income, health and poverty had all become concentrated in central Newquay and focused on poor quality private sector rented homes that were once larger bed and breakfast hotels and single homes. Many single people or families that were in and out of low paid jobs, surviving with poor health and sometimes with addiction problems, had all ended up in the popular town of Newquay.

So, Newquay still has much to be done beyond a new surf, yoga and vegan café image. Even in 2022 the local police were having to step up patrols to deal with drink-related anti-social behaviour in the town during the summer months. There are still the issues of decaying hotel and guest house sites that attract uncertain and poor-quality investment 'opportunities' to Newquay. Most sites seem to become anonymous blocks of apartments with few targeted on tackling the town's housing affordability crisis.

Let's go surfing… and to space!

The town's undoubted success as the premier surfing destination in the UK has brought a more 'relaxed' vibe to the resort but also another less welcome arrival: the van-lifers, parked up around the town, upsetting many local residents. Reports of anti-social behaviour and the long-term occupation of valuable parking spaces led the county council to consult on ways to restrict access to the town. Not every resident agrees it's an issue, however. The *I news* in January 2022 reported that some residents welcomed van-lifers as a part of Newquay's Cornish identity and pointed to van-life being a response to the local housing crisis as not everyone was an itinerant surfer.

Time to give the surfers a break. Ever since the early 1990s surfing culture has been important to the resort. Clothing labels such as Quiksilver and Fat Willy's brought surfing apparel to the young as the clothing of the moment. Surfing competitions promoted it as a sport and the search for the right 'breaks' and consistency led surfers to Fistral beach in particular. This beach faces west, with high twin headlands, exposing it to the sea and funnelling the Atlantic swells. At the northern end of the beach stands a natural reef called the Cribbar which makes waves break early, improving longevity. The beach became synonymous with surfing and as surfing schools, competitions, clothes shops and targeted cafes and restaurants expanded into Newquay, it rapidly became the best all year surfing resort in the UK.

The influence of Newquay as a surfer's town with a

growing youth culture brought the Extreme Sports Academy to Watergate Bay just up the Cornish coast, offering surfing, wave boarding, and paddle-boarding amongst other sports, for tuition and hire. It's a good example of how the town has used its assets to widen the employment offer away from pure tourism to a more diverse base built on its existing facilities. The Newquay airport is another example. Home to the Space Cluster, an Enterprise zone of aeronautics-based industries, it also hosts the Spaceport, where Virgin had intended to send satellites into space, clamped to a huge 747 areoplane that was to utilise the long airport runway. Unfortunately, and rather publicly, Virgin Orbit filed for bankruptcy after failing to secure rescue funding. Despite this knock the Spaceport has continued to work with global space and satellite businesses. The Spaceport itself already employs 150 staff with another 240 working across the local supply chain. The ambition is for the whole sector to bring in £1 billion of business to Cornwall by 2030.

Newquay goes bohemian

This type of new initiative is attracting plenty of new housing to Newquay too. The Duchy of Cornwall is a big landowner in the area and, guided by the new King's influence, a huge new housing development has attached itself to the town. It's designed to become a 'bohemian new town' of pastel-hued homes with a 'buzzing high street' all laid out in a rather wobbly grid pattern of Cornish named-streets. I quote from the Princes Foundation's own website which clearly wants to promote Nansledan, the name of the new town, as a sustainable, environmentally and economically friendly place. Occupying over

540 acres, the aim is to build 4,000 mixed-income homes over thirty years. The ambition is huge and welcome for Newquay, even if the development so far has a touch of the current King's nostalgia for toy-town terraces and pristine weirdness. Walking through it reminds you of the film *The Truman Show,* without the flowers or the residents.

The first Duchy scheme at Tregunnel Hill followed the principles of small-scale street scenes, front doors opening out directly onto streets and tightly controlled architectural character. It seems that Newquay is to be a giant test bed for not only controlling behaviour on its streets but also space travel and nostalgic twee architecture.

Wandering through Newquay the contrasts become clear. To be honest it's a bit of a mess. New flat-roofed blocks of flats sit amongst weather-battered Victorian and Edwardian homes many of which seem to be 'surf hotels'. Vegan cafes mix with boozy pubs and endless surf shops in an eclectic mix of totally unplanned styles that completely contrast with the ordered regime of Nansledan. Around the railway station the older decaying hotels are either closing down for redevelopment or struggling for life.

Down at the beaches surf schools and board shops are everywhere and irrespective of the weather there are crowds of youngsters dressed in wet suits carrying surfboards of every size imaginable. The beaches are wonderful though. Each one has a totally different character with Fistral being the main attraction as the surf pounds relentlessly eastwards.

So, I left Newquay in a mixed-up mood. It has got one of the English coast's best locations built around its terrific beaches, cliffs and headlands. The town is shapeless and in parts, downright trashy. But there is a lot going on in this far away part of the world, with the Duchy inspired new housing, the Virgin Spaceport and the growth of the surfing culture. So, give it a go and make your own mind up.

St Mawes, expensive, select and top of the poll

The journey is complete. From Skegness, bottom of the *Which?* pile for three years running, to St Mawes in deepest Cornwall, supposedly the best seaside resort in the country according to the *Which?* readers of 2020.

They loved the seafront, the scenery, the food and drink, the peace and quiet and the value for money on offer. Shopping and beach facilities were not so hot. Two stars for each but you wonder how they even got that score. The village doesn't really have much of a beach, other than a bit of rock-hopping fun along a sliver of sand that disappears at high tide and the shops are not going to set any retail-mad hearts a-flutter unless you are into watercolours and expensive clothes. What it does have is a select calmness, a stunning setting at the end of one of the headlands of the Roseland Peninsula, superb views and some well-known opportunities for high quality stopovers and exclusive dining. Truly the cod confit ending to the journey from the bag of chips in Skegness.

It's not a big place, in fact less than a thousand souls, but it trades on exclusivity, its bucolic charms and a waterside location that visitors and incomers love. The exclusivity comes through in the local house prices. The *Halifax Seaside Town Review* of house prices in 2021 showed the village had the eighth most expensive homes on the coast at an average sale price of

£501,638, but most astonishingly the biggest annual change. Prices had leapt up by 48% in just one year. A quick check of *Rightmove* found not one property for less than £595,000 and that was a small two bed cottage, admittedly on the waterfront. A few were available for over £2 million pounds.

MyLondon found out who was to blame. Incoming Londoners it seems, irrespective of the fact it's nearly 300 miles away, with the last twenty miles down country lanes. Locals complained of the village losing its identity and not being what it was forty years ago. Low wages in the hospitality sector, the lack of a diverse employment base and inadequate affordable housing had driven many local people out of the village. What was left was a surprisingly large number of bigger homes and not lots of the little terraced cottages of many Cornish villages. These were being snapped up by cash-rich incomers who would then, if they chose to, let out the homes at sky-high holiday let prices.

Back in 2010 *The Financial Times* was reporting the village had its first Russian and German buyers. In 2022 even the *Wall Street Journal* was spinning articles about the village's mad house prices.

I spoke to a local resident, who I dubbed 'Mr St Mawes' when I caught up with him, to talk through what was going on in the village. Phil Salter is well known in St Mawes and as well as appearing in a few media articles about the place he has played a starring role in a *Radio 4* podcast on changing house values. He immediately turned to the influx of new buyers into St Mawes as the biggest change he had seen in his many years in the village. In the past he has called them 'house farmers', churning properties for higher values or knocking down older homes on big plots to either build even bigger mansions or add two or three new homes to the plot. One group in the village did seem to benefit however: the sailing community. Phil felt that the sailors in St Mawes, both new and old, did manage to build and maintain a community, fashioned around the boatie lifestyle that you were either in or out of, locally.

Unashamedly chic and up-market

This demand was driven by, or supported by, dependent on your way of thinking, up-market hotels, pubs and restaurants settling in the village. St Mawes is home to the Tresanton Hotel owned by the Polizzi family of Rocco Forte and The *Hotel Inspector* TV fame. It's a former sailing club and now a thirty-room unobtrusive boutique hotel with its own yacht available to guests. Opened in 1998 it put St Mawes on the chic hotel and dining map by, in its own words, offering 'a slice of Mediterranean style' to Cornwall.

Competition in the chic and expensive category came from David Richards, at the time the Chairman of the Aston Martin car company, transforming the much older Idle Rocks hotel in 2013. Named 'Restaurant of the Year' and 'Best Small Hotel of the Year' in 2022 this hotel has certainly captured the quality market and has won a round of awards and plaudits since it opened. *Tatler Travel* even named it one of the 'sexiest hotels in the world' in 2018. Richards also owns the cheaper (I know reader, I stayed there) St Mawes Hotel right on the seafront.

Phil Salter, 'Mr St Mawes', welcomed the new hotels, calling them 'a credit to the village' and 'great employers'. He also liked the fact that they drew in wealthy spenders and celebrities despite the restaurant prices being out of his reach.

The arrival of these fancy new hotels saw the ultimate recognition for the village when a local bed and breakfast owner, Amelia Whitaker, persuaded Hasbro, the makers of the board game *Monopoly*, to produce a special St Mawes limited edition, with village locations replacing the likes of Mayfair and Bond Street. As the smallest place in the world to have its own *Monopoly* game you do have the chance to buy Tresanton and Idle Rocks yourself, as well as the local butchers.

It's not just the hotels that have gone up-market. The growing demand for high quality houses to rent for holiday staycations has a ready source in St Mawes with a large number of big and small lets available for well over £1,000 for the weekend. Yes, the weekend. Big money attracts big spending in shops too. Flashy galleries, clothes and jewellery shops pop up next to new cafes and restaurants whilst fish and chips and pub fare are catered for in the villages two pubs.

All of this has contributed to the village being called one of 'the hippest places in the UK' by *Travel Supermarket*, a price comparison website. Hipness appeared to be measured in terms of naturalism, vegan cafes, coffee and creativity so St Mawes' position is a bit of an anomaly. Hip, chic, or downright expensive, it's an odd one really because, to be honest, it's actually rather plain architecturally. Yes, there are some attractive cottages scattered higgledy-piggledy along the waterfront with fabulous views across the Carrick Roads to St Anthony and Falmouth but away from the water the village consists of a lot of anonymous large houses with big gardens oozing big money. In the wintertime that money slips away and the village slumps into a second home slumber.

The rise in second home ownership and with it, holiday letting, has become a real problem in this part of Cornwall. Analysis by the Cornwall County Council in 2021 showed the parish in which St Mawes sits had up to 32% second home ownership with almost 53% of homes without any usual resident.

Much of the local employment relies on low paid tourism jobs and finding affordable homes in the area has become increasingly difficult. Hospitality roles, dwindling fishing jobs and seasonal service employment does not bring in the type of money needed to buy £1 million houses. The whole peninsula is an Area of Outstanding Natural Beauty limiting the scope for development too. Once again local support has been needed to try and find a solution. A Roseland Community Land Trust (named after the peninsula) has been set up to purchase land and build rented homes for local people with a plan for a part council-owned site in St Mawes. Tight local eligibility criteria are applied by the Trust to ensure access for locally based applicants. It seems progress is grindingly slow, even when the site in question is right out on the edge of the village away from the horrendously expensive waterfront and despite local support, no houses are yet being built.

A village built on pilchards and a fort

Well before the big spenders arrived, St Mawes was regarded as an important enough spot by Henry VIII for him to promote the building one of the country's best preserved artillery forts. Together with Pendennis Castle across the Fal estuary, it was one of thirty forts built at the time of Henry VIII to protect important ports in the south from possible French or Spanish attacks.

The fort was built by a wealthy local Cornishman, Thomas Treffry, who benefitted financially from controlling extra taxes for Henry's war in France. Despite taking on the construction costs and the burden of maintaining a garrison he could also supervise the passage of ships with the captain of the Pendennis Castle.

St Mawes remained in military use from 1540 to 1956 and was periodically enlarged and reinforced with artillery as the threat level abroad increased. The castle is now in the hands of *English Heritage* and is one of the best preserved of its time.

The village of St Mawes owes its name to a visiting Saint, Maudez, who established a chapel by the Fal estuary in the fifth century. Nothing remains of it today as it was abandoned in the sixteenth century and decayed away. The village itself was a haven of pilchard fishing, now renamed Cornish sardines in an effort in 1997 to rebrand the common view of pilchards as cheap canned fish in tomato sauce. Many of the water-front buildings were given over to smokehouses, chandlers and fish stores. The great British painter J.M.W. Turner captured the waterfront scene in his painting *St Mawes at the Pilchard season* exhibited in 1812. At that time the Napoleonic Wars had stopped cross- Channel trade so much of the pilchard catch was turned into cheap manure.

The village would not have been a pleasant place during the pilchard season. The smell of the oily malodorous fish oil would have been overpowering in the summer, but the little fish brought money to the Cornish villages and the whole village would have been involved in its capture and treatment. At times there were so many they could be given away and this created a long-held stigma about the pilchard being a poor man's meal.

Phil Salter's home was previously used for fish curing and his once sloping floors helped the smelly oil to be washed straight out into the street.

Pilchard fishing declined in the twentieth century but is now making something of a small comeback under the banner of the Cornish sardine. St Mawes still has a few boats that fish the off-shore waters but in the past over twenty would sail out.

Today there is no strong-smelling fish oil to taint St Mawes as you stroll through the village. There is a lot of strolling going on too as the tourists emerge from the huge car park in the village centre or from the ferry from Falmouth or Truro. Whilst many of the village's buildings have been curated into a pristine state there are still the odd ones around waiting for new investment. Particularly so for the quayside home of the pilot gigs of St Mawes and the curious old petrol pumps that stand sentinel outside, advertising petrol at 2/3d a gallon. Pilot gigs would be used to guide ships into the harbour and have been a feature of the village since 1790. Now the Roseland Gig Club just row for fun.

And finally, what of my title to this book. Well, if Skegness is the bag of chips, then St Mawes is obviously the cod confit. Poor old Skegness, bottom of the *Which?* list is just full of chips and they are cheap too, perfectly capturing the essence of the resort and its charms. In St Mawes the food is much posher, equally reflecting the views of the *Which?* readers who dine in the Tresanton and Idle Rocks hotels. It's the place for your cod confit, crab tian and cioppino from £20 each and rising. It's a long way from two cod roe and chips for £4.95 at the Atlantic in Skegness.

CHAPTER FOURTEEN

Save our seaside

Britain's coast is in desperate trouble…
spare a thought for the 3.5 million who live on the coast all year
round - disproportionately poorer, iller, older, more mentally
depressed, in low-paid temporary work, more overweight
and more prone to suicide, drug abuse and self-harm
than if they lived just a few miles inland

Will Hutton in *The Guardian* in July 2021

Will Hutton doesn't hold back. But this is no attempt to bury the dying seaside resort. He goes on to say that the coast 'could and should become emblematic of health and vitality- a source of national pride'. He argues for the beautification of seafronts, for resorts becoming green energy hubs with new attractions and creative quarters, art and music colleges and more experimentation in spending and borrowing by central and local government.

All great ideas. It seems that he has been touring the coastal resorts with me.

I think he is on the right track. Yes, you will find poor health, deep poverty in concentrated areas, and an ageing population of retirees becoming older and iller, but these statistics need not define our resorts. My own simple tour has found a wealth of variety, initiative and creativity often initiated by local people who fully understand what is best for their areas. If anything, whilst big government spend, properly shaped locally, is always welcome, it's the micro-local ideas and investments that seem to hit home with the biggest impact. Attracting local entrepreneurs of the right sort, working to a long-term time-frame where local people and visitors buy in to a shared vision, seems to bring the real benefits.

But there are other things to discuss when we look at our seaside resorts today. What is the *learning* from my tour? What have I seen that has really made a local difference? Well, plenty actually: some positive, some negative, some strange, some downright weird. Let's run through what I have found in my own grand tour.

Not every smuggler was a loveable rogue

Why the love of smuggling? Why the romanticism and heroism with no smack of criminality? It was generally a vicious and nasty trade. Even so there are Smugglers Inns everywhere usually adorned with pictures of loveable rascals carrying a barrel of whiskey.

Paul Theroux remarked on the smuggling conundrum, noting that smugglers were often praised for recklessness and courage. Back in 1823 Robert Southey (quoted in the Lymington Museum) said 'there is danger in acting against smugglers and poachers, because smugglers think they have natural justice on their side. They therefore think themselves aggrieved when they are prosecuted for their illicit practices and feel as if they had the right to revenge themselves upon anyone who has taken part against them'.

Many of the older coastal villages and towns were smuggling havens well before the seaside visitors arrived. Beer, Lymington, Exmouth, Wells and Blakeney all had their fair share. Now their tales add a historical and romantic flourish to the older resorts. I think we need to be clear though. Not every smuggler was a raffish Robin Hood. Many were desperate and dangerous sorts and there is no point air-brushing this from history.

History, regeneration and affordability

Some resorts have an astonishingly long history and others, a pretty short one. Bamburgh, Blakeney, Wells, Hastings, Lymington and Beer were all ports or coastal settlements of varying importance hundreds of years ago. The focus of growth in these older resorts has changed of course, as time passes. Lymington owed its early wealth to salt, Blakeney and Wells to exports and imports through their ports, Spittal to the herring and salmon.

Compared to these places there are many others with a short history where growth was driven by single landowners, entrepreneurs and the arrival of the railway. Folkestone, Skegness, Hunstanton, Southsea and Weston-super-Mare are all just a couple of hundred years old at most.

As a result, these older villages and towns now tend to have the quaint cottages that were once the homes of fishermen. As time has passed their attractiveness has led to greater protection of their historical past and controls on development and change. Such places then become the havens of retirees and the better off, buying into once dilapidated homes, refurbishing as they go and driving values up.

Yesterday's slums have become today's second homes, host to Airbnb and holiday lets. A recent *Guardian* article pointed out that the number of 'entire places' to rent through Airbnb in coastal spots increased by 56% between 2019 and 2022. As day follows night the effect is to force out the poorly paid without the cash to buy into the rejuvenated villages. The cry to protect the historic, picturesque core kills off the potential to develop affordable homes and it is left to local people to think through ways to sustain a working settlement. All is not lost however and the initiative shown in places like Blakeney, Wells and St Mawes illustrates the point that local commitment can pay real dividends.

The power of the entrepreneurial spirit

Across the country, the power of the old landowners and entrepreneurs to create resorts with their influence and money was a big surprise to me. Individuals like Earl Radnor in Folkestone, Le Strange in Hunstanton, Lord Scarbrough in Skegness, Owen in Southsea and Unett in Filey, brought vision and enthusiasm to our seaside resorts and in many cases, single-handedly created the places we know today. They spotted the changing fashion amongst the wealthy for fresh air and seaside charms and threw themselves and their money at what, in many cases, were isolated, distant fishing villages with few prospects.

Many of these entrepreneurs were well connected too. If you could persuade any members of the Royal family to visit your burgeoning resort and give it a stamp of approval, then the exclusive status that followed brought fresh interest and affluent visitors. Resorts like Sidmouth, Weymouth and Folkestone all hugely benefitted from Royal entourages. Queen Victoria's purchase of Sandringham, near Hunstanton, turned the town's branch line into a Royal train connection and probably saved it from Beeching's axe too.

It is good to see modern day equivalents to these Victorian and Edwardian entrepreneurs emerging. Over in Folkestone Roger de Haan has made a huge impact in support of a wave of creativity and regeneration in the town. In Wells, it's the Holkham Hall effect and the investment of the Earl of Leicester that has seen a change to the way in which the local land has been managed and used to the benefit of hundreds of local people and the local environment. Down in Cornwall the Duchy of Cornwall is using its land and wealth to create sustainable environmentally friendly new housing. The Armstrongs of Bamburgh are restoring and revitalising the past in the village through their investment in the Castle and surrounding land.

Keep it local

It's not just well-off entrepreneurs that are investing in the seaside either. Local residents are doing it for themselves. In Hastings we have seen that the withdrawal of big funding, supporting grand initiatives like the Pier, the Jerwood and the University has led to more local investment regenerating the older shopping core and the seafront. Housing creativity has led to local people starting up small housing schemes through housing associations or community land trusts in Beer, Wells, Blakeney and St Mawes.

Attractive towns and villages often see local protection

societies emerge, including the oldest in England in Sidmouth. Many local museums rely upon resident initiative and generosity. Lymington, Weston-super-Mare, Hunstanton and Cromer all have excellent little showcases for their history and activities. Resident's groups have also been active across the resorts fighting off what they see as inappropriate developments that have often been proposed for much-loved long-standing hotels and residential sites. Exmouth, Newquay and Weymouth are all looking for big money investment into seafront sites that local people are seeking to control and protect.

The fragility of the national investment cycle and the twitchy decision-making of some private funders has often led to grandiose projects sweeping in... and then sweeping out, leaving resorts with big holes to fill. The real value of the Olympics to Weymouth remains an open debate. Banksy's intervention in Weston-super-Mare was welcomed but short-lived and it had a second temporary flourish with the See Monster. These resorts deserve better and the answer probably lies with initiatives that sustain value in the resorts, driven by local people, offering attractions and projects that are not so marginal in their profitability.

Uncertain future: call for 'Mr Seaside'

It is the case that some resorts know very clearly what their offer is and want to keep it that way. Skegness and Sidmouth are good examples. Skegness knows it is a vibrant, family driven and entertainment led resort without pretensions of exclusivity, grandiosity or picturesque charm. What you see is what you get and its visitors, many of whom are repeat customers, know what they will get.

Sidmouth offers something completely different: a sedate old-fashioned calm in its hotels, seafront, architecture and even its shops. There are no noisy rides or slot machines to disturb its bucolic charms and seafront promenading. Places like Blakeney, Bamburgh and Beer share this type of protected environment where there is no call for a brash funfair or arcade.

Other resorts seek something else. Trouble is, the search for the killer seaside solution can be a bit elusive or unclear? Bridlington thought a fancy new marina would do the trick, but it never arrived. Exmouth thinks that water-sports will bring in a different set of punters. Newquay has profited from surfing and a younger clientele. With Folkestone, it's art. Southsea mixes it up with Portsmouth's marine history. Others are a bit conflicted. Mind you, if you are such a resort, where there is a bit of doubt over your potential future, there is someone you can call. Wayne Hemingway and his creative team of consultants like nothing more than a call to arms to rescue this and that resort with their 'place-branding' consultancy.

Travelling round the coast, I became a bit conflicted myself over Wayne Hemingway's involvement. He seemed to pop up everywhere when a local council wanted a bit of fresh thinking and innovation. As 'Mr Seaside Resort' I'm not sure he always delivered and despite his best efforts to produce something both different and unique to each resort's requests, the ideas tended to be a bit repetitive; attract young people with money, bring in pop-up stalls, tone down the raucousness, tone up the creative independents, find the skateboarding hipsters. His clarion call is for towns to be brave, creative and receptive to new ideas. His own website says, 'you don't make change by taking the easy route'.

Weymouth, Hunstanton and Exmouth have all called for his help but there's little on the ground to show so far. His biggest success has been in Boscombe and Margate, but he has also been commissioned in Morecambe, Bognor Regis, Lowestoft, Bangor in Northern Ireland and most recently, Cleethorpes. A busy man.

Not all change is good: our changing coast and disappearing fish

Many of our seaside resorts began life as fishing villages with either beach drawn boats or small ports and quays. In the early years of tourism, fishing and resort activities operated side by side, often with the fishing action offering an attractive local activity for promenaders. We can see this happening up and down the coast in Spittal, Filey, Bridlington, Cromer, Hastings, Exmouth and Weymouth. But fishing is changing and not necessarily for the better for British fishermen. Declining fish stocks, competition from foreign fishing fleets of huge size and capacity, a strong feeling of post-Brexit betrayal of fishermen and politically promised reforms together with the sheer economic battle many fishing fleets have faced around our coast, has seen huge reductions in fishing trawlers and smaller boats in virtually every resort.

The response of many shrinking fleets has been to try and focus catches on local restaurants and sell direct to communities whilst also seeking out new markets. In Bridlington the lobster has become a major success story for its remaining fleet, in Cromer it's the crab and in Cornish villages, it's the newly branded Cornish sardine. The cobles of Filey and the small, beached boats of Beer and Hastings have now become tourist attractions too, drawing tourists into these resorts.

Many of the resorts we have visited have replaced or supplemented one type of boat, the fishing trawler, for another, the sailing yacht or ocean cruiser. Lymington and Weymouth have become a sailor's paradise and St Mawes benefits hugely from its monied sailing visitors. The marina at Exmouth has brought a different clientele to the old port and the quaint quays of Folkestone and Wells attract coastal and international sailors. Weymouth brings in the bigger cruise liners as well as smaller boats. All this activity works to change not just the economy of a resort but also its attractiveness to visitors and new residents. It's perhaps no surprise that Bridlington was so keen to bring a new marina to the town but also no surprise that not every resort can economically support such an investment.

As the centuries have passed it's not just the fishing that has changed. The entire coastline of Britain is changing too. Many resorts we have visited are exhibiting the effects of climate change and natural erosion writ large. The crumbling cliffs of Hunstanton and Sidmouth, the disappearing sands of Skegness, the coastal defence construction at Southsea, the possibility of Weymouth's ancient Sandsfoot Castle falling into the sea and the silting up of Blakeney and Wells are all real signs of a coast under strain and resorts are having to adapt to the different nature of the threat they face.

On a lighter note

Our seaside resorts have always tried to be fun places to visit.

Whether the smile on your face comes from the beauty of the scenery, the thrill of the funfair, the child on the donkey, the naughty postcards of Donald McGill or the taste of the candy floss, they have always sought to provide unique and compelling experiences that keep you coming back for more. I found our resorts to be full of surprises and eccentricity, much of it truly odd and of course, particularly British.

Only in our seaside resorts can we find the biggest joke shop and the biggest amateur tennis tournament in the world, unique end of pier shows, eccentric TV celebrities, wavy walls built by prisoners and authors, the first concrete underground car park, vast limestone caverns dating back to Roman times, museums with dinosaurs and sea-faring heroines and multi-level skateboard and BMX parks.

Perhaps these surprises are just a sign of the need for our resorts to accentuate their uniqueness and difference. Because we have so many, the competition for our money is fierce. Our resorts began their serious life once the railway arrived, bringing the closest big centres of population to their beaches in a few hours. Even today, resorts like Skegness and Bridlington continue to attract a long-standing loyal clientele from places like Nottingham, Leicester and Leeds. But the variety and number of resorts, coupled with the growing ease of travel meant visitors had plenty of choice, including going abroad.

Fun, eccentricities, surprising attractions, uniqueness and cultural variety have become much more important in today's competitive environment and Britain's resorts are full of it. So, let's enjoy the fun side of our resorts whilst encouraging the local politicians, entrepreneurs and innovators to invest for the long term in local buildings, attractions, businesses and the environment. Then we can begin to tackle the poverty and health issues that still plague our resorts with local dynamism and ideas at its heart.

Whither Which?

Perhaps a final word about our friends at *Which?* my unknowing guide to the seaside resorts of England. It's perhaps a bit too easy to smugly comment on the middle-class snootiness of much of the scoring by the magazine's readers. There is a clear love of fine scenery, peace and quiet and superb beaches. Noisy arcades, a welter of fish and chips and downmarket entertainment doesn't attract a lot of stars. There are some curious scores too. I have commented on how a couple of resorts don't have any beach access at all and yet still score well. One person's value for money is another's greasy burger joint too.

Over 4,000 people provide their views to *Which?* to produce the annual review and it certainly raises the profile of the magazine each time it comes out. All the local papers covering the top and the bottom scoring resorts, relay the story, usually accompanied by welcoming/distraught politicians giving their views on the fantastic/abysmal position of their resort.

Does it matter? All I would say is, let's just treat it as a bit of fun, a part of the eccentricity of our resorts and our love of the list. I'm thankful to *Which?* for launching me into this book and giving me the idea to get out and about around the coast. Just leave Skegness alone next year.

Bibliography

Chapter One

www.coastaltourismacademy.co.uk

Which? Guide to the best seaside resorts in the UK 2020.

Fury over Which? survey rating Skegness as worst resort in UK, Skegness Standard, 21st July 2020.

Skegvegas is the best; Lincolnshire reacts to resort voted worst in UK, The Lincolnite, 21st July 2020.

Skegness ranked as worlds 9th worst holiday destination, itv. Com 22nd January 2017.

Skegness voted best place in UK to visit by car, Skegness Standard, 29th August 2020.

Wish you were here: England on Sea, Travis Elborough, 2010.

The interplay of health, pleasure and wellness in British seaside resorts: the case of Skegness on the Lincolnshire coast, Mohammed Chamekh, 2019.

The Nations Host: Butlins and the story of the British seaside, Kathryn Ferry, 2016.

The British Seaside Holiday, Kathryn Ferry, 2009.

The British Seaside: holidays and resorts in the twentieth century, John Walton, 2000.

Designing the Seaside: Architecture, Society and Nature, Fred Gray, 2009.

Rediscovering cultural tourism: cultural regeneration in seaside towns, James Kennell, 2010.

An asset and a challenge: heritage and regeneration in coastal towns in England, English Heritage, 2007.

England's seaside resorts, English Heritage, 2007.

The Kingdom by the Sea, Paul Theroux, 1983.

The Seaside Tourist Industry in England and Wales: Employment, economic output, location and trends, Christina Beatty, Steve Fothergill, Tony Gore and Ian Wilson, 2010.

Chief Medical Officers Annual Report 2021: Health in Coastal Communities, Chief Medical Officer for England, 2021.

Living on the edge: Britain's coastal communities, Social Market Foundation, 2017.

An Asset and a Challenge; Heritage and Regeneration in Coastal Towns in England, English Heritage, 2007.

The return of the Great British seaside, National Geographic, April 2018.

With tourism booming, Great Yarmouth dreams of turning the tide, The Guardian, September 2021.

Chapter Two

The National Piers Society: Skegness, www.piers.org.uk

Skegness name change suggested by tourism expert. BBC news January 2012.

Skegness uses images of Blackpool and Brighton to promote resort, BBC News, June 2012.

Beside the Seaside, edited by Ruth Petrie, 2009.

Wish you were here: England on Sea, Travis Elborough 2010.

Wish EU were here, The New European, November 2022.

Seaside Resorts, Candida Lycett Green, 2011.

Skegness, Winston Kime, 2006.

The Road to Little Dribbling: More notes from a small island, Bill Bryson, 2015.

Skegness pier to be extended five times longer and restored to its former Victorian era glory, Leicester Mercury, July 2021.

Connected Coast Board Town Investment Plan, October 2020.

The future of seaside towns, Select Committee on Regenerating Seaside towns and communities, report of session 2017-2019.

Chapter Three

Reflections on the Lynn and Hunstanton railway line fifty years on, Ben Colson, Hunstanton Town and Around, May 2019.

Scandal-on-Sea: HG Wells, his lover and their secret Norfolk hideaway, Eastern Daily Press, September 2016.

www.hunstantonrail.org.uk

A Monarchs Line, M.R.Windle, www.wolfertonroyalstation.co.uk

Pier centre has £4.25m price tag for new owner, www.yourlocalpaper.com, August 2015.

School at Hunstanton, Norfolk by Alison and Peter Smithson, Philip Johnson, Architectural Review, August 1954.

The New Brutalism, Reyner Banham, Architectural Review, December 1955.

Hunstanton Neighbourhood Development Plan 2020-2036, February 2021.

Wayne Hemingway to redesign Hunstanton seafront, Eastern Daily Press, June 2018.

Wimbledon-on-Sea, Ashley Martin, 2021.

Chapter Four

Have you heard about Blakeney, Peter Brooks, 2001.

Beside the Seaside, edited by Ruth Petrie, 2009.

A port in decline; Blakeney and Cley 1850-1914, Jonathan Hooton, The Glaven Historian, 2004.

High Society, Inside Housing, January 2006.

Sixty years of village housing and conservation, Blakeney Neighbourhood Housing Society, 2011.

www.Blakeneyhousing.org.uk

Blakeney Neighbourhood Plan 2020-2040.

Don't need the sunshine, John Osborne, 2013.

www.wellsguide.com

Holkham estate hiring warden- with tasks to include nudist beach patrol, Eastern Daily Press, February 2021.

Popular railway will cease to exist as soon as this year, Fakenham and Wells Times, May 2021.

www.holkham.co.uk

Holkham Gazette, Spring/summer 2021.

www.homesforwells.com

Wells Coastal Community Team, www.coastalcommunities.co.uk, February 2017.

Chapter Five

Jarrolds Illustrated Guide to Cromer and Neighbourhood, 1897.

The Kingdom by the Sea, Paul Theroux, 1983.

www.literarynorfolk.co.uk/cromer

Head shaking over Cromer's future really is nothing new, Keith Skipper in the Eastern Daily Press, 2018.

www.cromerpier.co.uk

Cromer crabs-feeling the pinch, Fishing News, September 2019.

Fishermen should grow up- report sparks clash over crab fishery, Eastern Daily Press, May 2021.

Sir James Dyson's latest gift to Norfolk is funding towards a new Coastwatch station, North Norfolk News, June 2019.

Chapter Six

Guide to Exmouth: Sunny Resort of the West, Exmouth Advertising committee information bureau, 1914.

Exmouth visitor survey 2016, East Devon District Council, 2016

www.saveExmouthseafront.Wordpress.Com

Desire expressed to 'get seafront done' for controversial Exmouth site, www.exmouth.nub.news October 2020.

Power and Politics at the Seaside: the development of Devon's resorts in the twentieth century, Nigel Morgan and Annette Pritchard, 1999.

www.exmouthhistory.co.uk

The rise of the Devon seaside resorts 1750-1900, John Travis, 1993.

Rolle College, Exmouth, www.hansard.parliament.uk July 2008.

Chapter Seven

Beer in Time and Tide, Arthur Chapple, 1987.

Beer microbes live 533 days outside ISS, BBC, August 2010.

Smuggling in the British Isles, Richard Platt, 2007.

www.honitonlace.com

The tourist and visitor guide to Sidmouth and its neighbourhood, Whittaker and Co. 1845.

Sidmouth: a history, Sid Vale Association, revised edition 2015.

Sidmouth People and Places, Nigel Hyman (Sid Vale Association), revised edition 2015.

The rise of the Devon seaside resorts 1750-1900, John Travis, 1993.

www.sidvaleassociation.org.uk

www.thedonkeysanctuary.org.uk

Chapter Eight

Bridlington is one of the best places to live in England, Hull and East Yorkshire News, February 2021.

Bridlington- the popular seaside resort now ranked as one of the most deprived places in Britain, Yorkshire Post, July 2021.

Bridlington History tour, Mike Hitches, 2020.

www.Bridlingtonheritage.com

Bridlington, Ian and Margaret Sumner, 2001.

Beside the seaside; a history of Yorkshire's seaside resorts, John Heywood, 2017.

Yorkshire port aims to be the 'Lobster Capital of Europe', Fishing News, August 2020.

Yorkshire lobster exporter says Brexit costs have forced it to close, The Guardian, February 2021.

www.thefileyfishermenschoir.co.uk

Filey: from fishing village to Edwardian resort, Michael Fearon, 2008.

A history of the Butlins railways, Peter Scott, 2001.

www.butlins-memories.com

Filey could be partially underwater in 50 years study reveals, The Press, June 2022.

Chapter Nine.

Lymington named as one of the best places to live, Bournemouth Echo, March 2018.

Is Lymington the snootiest town in Britain, The Guardian, September 2010.

Lymington: the town that's too posh for Argos turns against Wetherspoon's pubs, The Independent, October 2011.

Lymington's wavy walls, Lymington Society and Residents Association, 1991.

Secret Lymington, Aimee Durnell, 2013.

Royal Lymington Yacht Club 1922-1972, RLYC publication, 1972.

On the Slow Train Again, Michael Williams, 2012.

Lymington: an illustrated history, Jude James, 2007.

Southsea: it's story, William Curtis, 1978.

Struggle and Suffrage in Portsmouth: Women's Lives and the Fight for Equality, Sarah Quail, 2018.

Selling Southsea, Promoting Portsmouth, 1920-2000, Nigel Yates, 2002.

Sunny Southsea: illustrated guide to Southsea and Portsmouth, edited by A.R. Holbrook, 1899.

The growth of Southsea as a Naval Satellite and Victorian resort, Dr R.C. Riley, 1972.

Portsmouth and the Visitor economy, Report to Portsmouth City Council, September 2018.

The Geography of Defence, edited by Michael Bateman and Raymond Riley, 1987.

Chapter Ten

www.bamburghresearchproject.co.uk

Bamburgh and the Farne Islands, Frank Graham, 1991.

www.lordcrewescharity.org.uk

www.bamburghcastlegolfclubco.uk

We're being overrun by tourists… we're just too popular, Mailonline, May 2022

Berwick-on-Tweed: three places, two nations, one town, Adam Menuge with Catherine Dewar, 2009.

www.spittalisgreat.co.uk

Early Victorian Spittal, Michael Cullen, 2005.

Secret Spittal, Spittal Improvement Trust, 2020

Chapter Eleven

The new Illustrated Handbook to Folkestone and its picturesque neighbourhood, Hamilton, Adams and Co, 1848.

Folkestone and Hythe District Heritage Strategy, 2018.

Modernism on Sea, edited by Lara Feigel and Alexandra Harris, 2009.

Why Folkestone is Kent's most underestimated seaside town, Harpers Bazaar, 2021.

Arts-led Regeneration and Community Cohesion: a study of Folkestone, Kent, James Kennell, 2007.

Folkestone hit by gentrification row over Saga tycoon's harbour plan, The Guardian, August 2016.

The Roger de Haan Charitable Trust, www.rdhct.org.uk

www.creativefolkestone.org.uk

Case study: Folkestone Creative Quarter, National Coastal Tourism Academy, 2018.

A town that is weird in so many ways, www.hastingsindependentpress.co.uk, December 2017.

Is it the end of the pier for Hastings? The Guardian, March 2019.

Walking on water or lost at sea: Hastings split over its people's pier, The Guardian, July 2018.

www.piers.org.uk

Jerwood Gallery to lose collection in dispute with funder, Museums Journal, February 2019.

Jerwood Gallery to rebrand as Hastings Contemporary, www.artlyst.com, March 2019.

Local uproar as University of Brighton announces withdrawal from Hastings, www.Hastingsindependentpress.co.uk March 2016.

Campus closure not the end of Hastings ambition to be a University town, Hastings in Focus, August 2019.

Sussex fishing community gets a taste of Brexit betrayal, Sussex Bylines, January 2021.

Fishing for a new future, www.Hastingsindependentpress.co.uk, July 2020.

EU funds welcomed by fishing community, www.hastingsindependentpress.co.uk , July 2019.

www.wrnv.org.uk

The America Ground, www.hastingsindependentpress.co.uk , December 2016.

How Sidney Little made his mark on Hastings, The Argus, July 2013.

From land and sea the iconic structure that defines the St Leonards seafront, www.hastingsindependentpress.co.uk , October 2021.

Chapter Twelve

A Kingdom by the Sea, Paul Theroux, 1983.

20 best coastal towns to move to in the UK, Country Living, April 2021.

Quarter of Weymouth and Portland houses sold as second homes, Dorset Echo, February 2019.

The 30 best seaside towns in the UK to discover in 2022, www.roughguides.com

Weymouth and Portland amongst 10% most deprived areas of the UK, Dorset Echo, October 2019.

Sun, sand and inequality: why the British seaside towns are losing out. The Guardian, June 2014.

Weymouth-Viva Las Weygas, www.chillisauce.com

Weymouth's seaside heritage, Brodie, Ellis, Stuart and Winter, English Heritage, 2008.

Perfidious Weymouth; Portland's 2012 Olympic Sailing story, www.building.co.uk November 2008.

The Portland Plan: Neighbourhood Plan for Portland 2017-2031. January 2020

Jurassica dinosaur museum £80m project scrapped, BBC News, October 2017

www.edenportland.org

New development planned at former QinetiQ site, Newtons Cove, Weymouth, Dorset Echo, July 2021.

Calls to breathe new life into Weymouth amid worries seaside towns are being left behind, Dorset Echo, April 2019.

Wayne Hemingway working on Weymouth seafront enhancement, Dorset Echo, May 2022.

www.tropicanaweston.co.uk

Transformation plan for Weston's empty town centre buildings, www.somersetlive.co.uk, April 2022.

www.westonwintergardens.co.uk

Weston-super-Mare: a Victorian seaside town, Historic England, 2020.

Weston-super-Mare: Prospectus for Change, North Somerset Council, 2015.

Chapter Thirteen

www.historichotelsthenandnow.com

Newquay reinvented: 'You stopped finding knickers in your garden' BBC News, December 2019.

A night out in Magaluf UK, The Mirror, July 2017.

How deprivation and drugs helped make this area of Newquay one of the poorest in Britain, Cornwall Live, October 2017.

Newquay police introduce special patrols to crack down on anti-social behaviour, CornwallLive, July 2022.

Newquay tries to ban people living in vans after complaints from the Cornish town's residents, I news, January 2022.

The history of surfing in Newquay, Cornwall,
www.cornishwave.com

www.cornwallspacecluster.co.uk

Halifax Seaside Town Review, 2021.

Idle Rocks owners buy St Mawes Hotel, www.bighospitality.co.uk.

Join the millionaires in one of the region's most exclusive haunts, ITV News, March 2012.

The 14 sexiest hotels in the world, www.tatler.com , February 2018.

Uk Property: why St Mawes stands out from the rest of Cornwall, Financial Times, November 2013.

Englands coastal villages are quaint and charming. Second homeowners are taking the bait, Wall Street Journal, July 2022.

www.roselandclt.org

Chapter Fourteen

There is a way to save our coastal resorts... welcome to Zoomtown-on-Sea, Will Hutton, The Guardian, July 2021.

Death of many big hotels as holiday traits change, The Guardian, 18 October 2022.

Also by this author

This is Paul Doe's third book. His previous books, also published by the Conrad Press, were *Dividing up the World; the true story of our international borders and why they are where they are* and *My Neighbour over the Border; tales of towns and cities separated by borders and how they get along.*

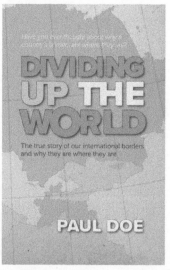

*Dividing up the World; the true story of our international
borders and why they are where they are*
ISBN 978-1-913567-04-0

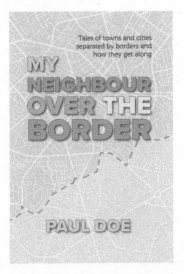

My Neighbour over the Border; tales of towns and cities separated by borders and how they get along.
ISBN 978-1-914913-08-2

They are available from amazon, amazon kindle, from all good bookshops and from The Conrad Press Ltd. website www.theconradpress.com